PENGUIN CLASSICS

LIFE IS A DREAM

PEDRO CALDERÓN DE LA BARCA was one of the leading dramatists of the Spanish Golden Age. He was born in Madrid on
January 17, 1600. His father was Secretary to the Royal Treasury and a minor noble, and his mother was a devoutly religious
woman who died when he was a child. Calderón studied canon
law in preparation for his presumed career in the church, but in
the 1620s he started to write verse, and his success in competitions attracted attention. The first known staging of one of his
plays was a 1623 performance of *Amor, honor, poder* (Love,
Honor, and Power). Eventually, the prolific Calderón would write
approximately 120 full-length dramatic works, some 80 one-act
autos sacramentales (religious mystery plays), and many other
short pieces of poetry and works for the theater. In 1636 King
Philip IV named him a knight of the Order of Santiago. His output lessened in the 1640s, and in 1651 Calderón entered the
priesthood, becoming chaplain of the Capilla de los Reyes
Nuevos at the cathedral in Toledo, and then, in 1656, head of the
congregation of San Pedro in Madrid. He continued to write both
secular and religious plays until his death on May 25, 1681.

GREGARY J. RACZ is associate professor in the Department of
Foreign Languages and Literature at Long Island University,
Brooklyn. His translation of the mock-Renaissance farce *Rig-
maroles* appeared in *Three Comedies,* his edited volume of plays
by the contemporary Spanish dramatist Jaime Salom. A specialist
in poetic translation, Racz has published works by the Cuban
writer José Lezama Lima, the Peruvian Eduardo Chirinos, and the
Argentine experimental XUL group.

PEDRO CALDERÓN DE LA BARCA

Life Is a Dream

(LA VIDA ES SUEÑO)

Translated with an Introduction by
GREGARY J. RACZ

PENGUIN BOOKS

PENGUIN BOOKS

Published by the Penguin Group
Penguin Group (USA) Inc., 375 Hudson Street, New York, New York 10014, U.S.A.
Penguin Group (Canada), 90 Eglinton Avenue East, Suite 700, Toronto, Ontario, Canada M4P 2Y3
(a division of Pearson Penguin Canada Inc.)
Penguin Books Ltd, 80 Strand, London WC2R 0RL, England
Penguin Ireland, 25 St Stephen's Green, Dublin 2, Ireland (a division of Penguin Books Ltd)
Penguin Group (Australia), 250 Camberwell Road, Camberwell, Victoria 3124, Australia
(a division of Pearson Australia Group Pty Ltd)
Penguin Books India Pvt Ltd, 11 Community Centre, Panchsheel Park, New Delhi–110 017, India
Penguin Group (NZ), cnr Airborne and Rosedale Roads, Albany, Auckland 1310, New Zealand
(a division of Pearson New Zealand Ltd)
Penguin Books (South Africa) (Pty) Ltd, 24 Sturdee Avenue, Rosebank, Johannesburg 2196, South Africa

Penguin Books Ltd, Registered Offices:
80 Strand, London WC2R 0RL, England

This translation first published in Penguin Books 2006

5   7   9   10   8   6   4

Translation and introduction copyright © Gregory J. Racz, 2006
All rights reserved

CAUTION: This drama in its printed form is dedicated to the reading public only. Professional and amateur performance, motion picture, radio and television broadcasting rights, and other rights in it are strictly reserved to the translator, Gregory J. Racz. No performance, professional or amateur, broadcast, nor public reading may be given without written permission in advance. Address inquiries concerning performance and production rights to Gregory J. Racz, Department of Foreign Languages and Literature, Long Island University, Brooklyn, One University Plaza, Brooklyn, New York 11201.

LIBRARY OF CONGRESS CATALOGING IN PUBLICATION DATA
Calderón de la Barca, Pedro, 1600-1681.
[Vida es sueño. English]
Life is a dream = La vida es sueño / Pedro Calderón de la Barca ; translated with an introduction
by Gregory J. Racz.
p. cm.
ISBN 978-0-14-310482-7
I. Racz, Gregory Joseph. II. Title. III. Title: Vida es sueño.
PQ6292.V513 2007
862'.3—dc22   2006043496

Printed in the United States of America
Set in Sabon

Contents

Introduction

Pedro Calderón de la Barca's path to literary fame as Spain's pre-eminent Golden Age dramatist was far more direct than his circuitous road to the priesthood. Born in Madrid on January 17, 1600, to a father of minor nobility serving as Secretary to the Royal Treasury and a pious mother whose dream was that her second surviving male child enter the church, Calderón should have been on a career trajectory predetermined by birth order. His older brother, Diego, by the societal logic of the time, was dutifully bound to inherit his father's position while the younger, José, would become a military officer; their sister, Dorotea, was dispatched to a convent at the tender age of thirteen. Young Pedro was only ten, and a student at the city's excellent Jesuit-run Colegio Imperial, when his beloved mother died—the first of a series of childhood tragedies that would derail his intended assumption of a family-endowed chaplaincy. Shortly after becoming a widower, Calderón's father married a woman who cared little for her stepchildren. In 1614, Pedro continued his studies at the Universidad de Alcalá outside Madrid. When his father passed away in 1615, he left a will that contained a clause urging Pedro to follow the path expected of him, and the Calderón children were looked after largely by a maternal uncle. Pedro studied canon law in pursuit of his vocation at the Universidad de Salamanca until 1618, when, probably as a result of the family's reduced economic circumstances, he was temporarily excommunicated for his failure to pay rent to the convent in which he lodged, and was held for a time in the university prison.

Two events of the 1620s point to an early adulthood at odds with his widely acknowledged qualities of charity, responsibility, and collegiality later in his life. Though details are sketchy, it is known that all three Calderón brothers sought refuge in the Austrian embassy in 1621 after the violent death of Nicolás de Velasco, the son of a man in the Duke of Frías's service, and that this affair was settled with a hefty monetary payment raised by the sale of Diego's title to their deceased father's position. In 1629, an attack on one of Calderón's brothers forced the assailant to seek refuge in a Trinitarian convent, where the surreptitious removal of nuns' veils by his overly zealous pursuers caused a minor scandal famously denounced by a fiery preacher of the day. It was during this decade, though, that evidence of Calderón's first successful attempts at writing come to light in the verse he composed for competitions held to honor Madrid's patron saint, Isidore. His submissions attracted the attention of no less a luminary than Lope Félix de Vega Carpio, the reigning playwright of the day, who praised the young writer for his skill and grace. Calderón would go on to place third in the contests of 1622. While biographical information on Calderón is occasionally as imprecise as the chronology of his manuscripts, the first recorded performance of a play, *Amor, honor, poder* (Love, Honor, and Power), dates from 1623. Over the course of a long and extremely productive career, Calderón would write approximately 120 full-length dramatic works, some 80 one-act *autos sacramentales* commemorating the divine mysteries of the Eucharist, and other short pieces of poetry and works for the theater. His copious output was greatly encouraged by the patronage of King Philip IV, who commissioned works for a new palace theater and named Calderón a knight of the Order of Santiago in 1636.

By the 1635 composition of *La vida es sueño* (Life Is a Dream), a work many hold to be the supreme example of Spanish Golden Age drama, Calderón had completed a varied body of work for the theater that includes the majority of the plays for which he remains best known. While dates are sometimes approximate, comedies such as *La dama duende* (The Phantom

Lady) and *Casa con dos puertas mala es de guardar* (A House with Two Doors Is Difficult to Guard) were written in 1629; the drama of Christian sacrifice *El príncipe constante* (The Constant Prince) and the semimystical *La devoción de la cruz* (Devotion to the Cross) were finished the following year. In 1632, Calderón published his first play, *El astrólogo fingido* (The Fake Astrologer), a comedy that inspired adaptations by such world-renowned writers as France's Thomas Corneille, England's John Dryden, and Germany's Johann Ludwig Tieck. The murder of a wife, an incorrectly designated "Spanish" theme with which Calderón remains doggedly identified, lies at the heart of two dramas also written around this time, *El médico de su honra* (The Surgeon of His Honor) and *A secreto agravio, secreta venganza* (Secret Vengeance for Secret Insult), the former set in an earlier era and the latter in a foreign country. Sometime between 1635 and 1637 Calderón also wrote *El gran teatro del mundo* (The Great Theater of the World), widely considered his finest *auto;* the equally notable honor play *El alcalde de Zalamea* (The Mayor of Zalamea); and *El mágico prodigioso* (The Wonder-Working Magician), a delightfully lyrical work loosely based on the Faust legend.

In the 1640s, at the height of Calderón's professional standing and prestige at court, a series of unfortunate events constricted his burgeoning theatrical output. A revolt in the province of Catalonia against centralized Spanish rule obliged Calderón in his capacity as knight of the Order of Santiago to fight in two campaigns against the rebel armies, and in 1642 he returned to Madrid wounded. The death in 1644 of Isabel, Philip IV's queen, shuttered the theaters for an observance of national mourning. The personal tragedy of his brother José's death in battle followed in 1645, a year before the untimely death of Baltasar Carlos, the heir apparent to the Spanish throne, which closed the theaters once again, this time from 1646 to 1649. During this period, his other brother, Diego, also died, as did the mother of Calderón's illegitimate son, whom he recognized and provided for throughout his life. These sudden emotional and professional setbacks may have occasioned a period of midlife reflection in Calderón, intensified perhaps by increased economic difficulties. Whatever the case, the many detours on Calderón's road to the priesthood ended in 1651, when he at last took holy orders, becoming chaplain of the Capilla de los Reyes Nuevos at the cathedral in Toledo. From this time until his death on May 25, 1681, Calderón dedicated his theatrical talents almost entirely to the production of *autos*. Possibly to figure more prominently in the theatrical life of the capital, Calderón returned to Madrid in 1656 to head the congregation of San Pedro. There, in this final phase of his professional life, he wrote additional mythological plays, a few works set to music, and the occasional secular comedy.

Lope de Vega's death in 1635, the year *Life Is a Dream* was written, all but cemented Calderón's position as the leading Spanish playwright of the day. The last of Calderón's challengers to this unofficial claim was Tirso de Molina, author of the Don Juan play *El burlador de Sevilla* (The Trickster of Seville), who died in 1648. By then, the Spanish baroque stage had lost such greats as Pérez de Montalván (d. 1638), Ruiz de Alarcón (d. 1639), and Mira de Amescua (d. 1644). Inheriting the mantle of Lope de Vega, the man Miguel de Cervantes called *"el monstruo de naturaleza"* (the prodigy of nature) for having written more than seven hundred plays, Calderón would come to be dubbed *"el monstruo de ingenio"* (the prodigy of invention) for his perfection of the three-act dramatic structure and mixed versification Lope had both instituted and popularized for a nascent national theater.

While tales of the sleeper transported had appeared for centuries in Western and non-Western cultures alike, critics have noted that *Life Is a Dream* bears more than a passing resemblance to Ludovicus Hollonius's play *Somnium vitae humanae* (1605), written in German despite its Latin title, although no direct line of influence has been established between these works. The story of a drunkard who is turned into the Duke of Bourgogne before resuming his natural state invites compelling comparisons with Calderón's masterpiece. So, too, does the author's own *Yerros de naturaleza y aciertos de fortuna* (Nature's Errors Redeemed by Fortune), co-written in 1634 with Antonio Coello, in which the relationships and experiences of a royal family seem a sort of preliminary sketch for the work Calderón wrote the following year. The emerging canon of the Spanish Renaissance theater, however, contained little that could prepare for Calderón's intricately woven handling of this theme in *Life Is a Dream*, a highly poetic drama of free will versus predestination and of nature's versus nurture's role in self-determination played out against the backdrop of court intrigue and the restoration of personal honor.

Life Is a Dream relates the story of Prince Segismund's spiritual redemption and improbable assumption of the Polish throne. Heartlessly imprisoned from birth by his father, King Basil, a devotee of astrology who had divined in the stars that an ungodly son would one day place his heel upon his sire's head, Segismund is reared in nearly savage isolation, attended only by the fitfully pitiless Clotaldo. Rosaura, a Russian noblewoman on a quest to demand satisfaction of the nobleman who has deceived her, accidentally stumbles upon the rightful heir's rustic cell on the eve of the prince's return to court. There, the putatively childless king has decided to determine whether human beings can contravene the dictates of the heavens. Having ordered the prince drugged to ensure his ready transport, Basil allows his uncultivated son to interact freely with the nobles and servants at the palace. In the meantime, Astolf, the nephew Basil plans to name the next king of Poland, is revealed to be the deceitful suitor who has abandoned Rosaura.

Astolf's subsequent wooing of his cousin Stella, Basil's choice for Poland's next queen, is complicated by the sudden appearance of Rosaura, now disguised at court as one of Stella's ladies-in-waiting on the advice of Clotaldo, who has realized that she is the child he abandoned when leaving Russia for Poland as a young man. Segismund develops a strange attraction to Rosaura, and takes a liking to her former manservant, Clarion, who comes to function as the rightful prince's hapless valet and erstwhile jester. When Basil's ill-conceived experiment in unrestrained behavior yields predictably disastrous results, Segismund is drugged again and unceremoniously taken back to languish in his cell. There, Clotaldo informs the prince that all he believes he has experienced was nothing more than a dream, and Segismund despairs of deliverance until Basil's Polish subjects learn of his existence and revolt in support of proper royal succession. The resolution of these various subplots and the fates of the characters involved rest ultimately upon the battle for monarchical succession waged at the play's end, in which political fortunes are not strictly adjudicated by the standards of personal worthiness found in conventional morality.

A truly singular figure in the canon of Western literature, Segismund attains critical insight into the importance of maintaining a nobility of spirit after successive stages of suffering, resignation, and reflection. These trials of a human soul, individualistic though they may appear, are nevertheless played out within a context of competing universal philosophies, ideologies, and worldviews. This may surprise readers expecting to find a traditional Judeo-Christian cosmogony informing the action of the play. While the predominantly Catholic Spain of 1635 had grown accustomed to the doctrinal rigors of the Inquisition, established in 1478 to eradicate Jewish heresy but increasingly used by Philip IV's father to combat the spread of Calvinism, and while Spanish royalty and Calderón held orthodox Catholic beliefs, *Life Is a Dream* seems more imbued with pagan Greek and Roman values than with a staunch Christian faith. The play's fleeting mentions of Christ's crucifixion, the Catholic Church's calendar, sacred skits, oaths to God, and the un-Christian belief in fatalism, for example, pale beside the numerous references to mythological and historical figures from classical antiquity. Within this ambient paganism, critics are correct to note a Platonist sensibility in a plot revolving around the ungodly "science" of astrology, as well as in Segismund's unschooled response to female beauty and the apparent innateness of his latently "magnanimous" character. Whether the prince is better viewed as an analogue to Prometheus, severely punished by the gods for the threat of usurping their sovereign powers, or to Adam, a new man fallen from an edenic life though destined to have dominion over a lesser land, is open to debate. In either case, these apparent tensions between conflicting worldviews in Calderón's play are smoothed over through the rationalizations of medieval scholasticism, a theological and philosophical method that sought to bridge the myriad chasms between classical pagan culture and Catholicism by integrating Aristotelian and Platonic thought with Christian teachings. The resulting hybridization of the work's textual universe is typical of the Renaissance mind's ability to accommodate such obvious incongruities.

Still, it is neither Catholicism nor paganism but so-called natural law, elements of which may be found in both of these ontological systems, that takes primacy in the ethical framework selectively governing the characters and events in *Life Is a Dream*. As manifested in the relationships among human beings in families, society, and politics, natural law broadly unites the play's competing worldviews under the moral imperatives (also shared at least in theory by the chivalric codes of the aristocracy) of goodness, mercy, justice, and virtue. Basil, for example, is a reprehensible if slightly ridiculous figure not because of his fatuous belief in astrology, but because he is an inhumane, unnatural father who has robbed his son of a tolerable existence and the Polish people of their rightful heir through natural succession by primogeniture. Similarly, Segismund, though marginally catechized by Clotaldo, derives the bulk of his learning and understanding of the world not from church doctrine but from direct observations of nature. Before the prince can assume the throne for which he is destined, he must learn the universally ennobling values of prudence and forgiveness. In a textual world only nominally Christian, what besides an abiding belief in the intrinsic importance of benevolence would compel Clotaldo to urge a prison-bound Segismund to perform good deeds regardless of whether he believes life is reality or dream? Salvation in a traditionally religious sense resonates weakly among such competing ideologies. Following the heraldic strictures of a divinely ordained order giving primacy to bloodline and caste, the actions at the Polish court inevitably lead to the resolution of dramatic conflict in accordance with the law of nature: a father and son are duly reconciled; an intermittently heartless tutor is pardoned for his shortcomings; a rebellious soldier is imprisoned for treason; a woman's honor is restored through an acknowledgment of past transgression when Astolf weds Rosaura (though only after her noble status has been confirmed); and the prince marries the abandoned Stella, thereby ensuring a final orderly pairing and the ultimate return of the king's son to the throne. Reflecting the slow trajectory of this recovery of essential goodness and innate nobility, the "wild"— that is, unnatural—horse/hippogriff mentioned in the first line of Life Is a Dream tellingly yields the stage to Segismund's "prudent and judicious" prince at play's close.

The work's prevailing metaphysics aside, Segismund's progressive transformations from noble savage to brutish courtier to enlightened monarch may strike a discordant note in audiences unfamiliar with pre-Romantic conceptualizations of character. Segismund's scripted, somewhat hasty conversions reflect the Spanish Golden Age aesthetic that relegates individual psychology to a secondary plane and conceives of personality as subservient to the conventional exigencies of plot, theme, and structure. This approach to characterization is, perhaps, best viewed in the baroque tension of competing identities each protagonist subsumes in somewhat stilted fashion within a dual self. Segismund, as mentioned above, is both abject prisoner and exalted prince, "a man of a beast / [a]nd a beast of a man," as he declares in the play's best-known chiasmus—a "mongrel mix," as he elsewhere describes this ontological dialectic. Basil is both superstitious and learned, a gullible astrologer and a concerned (if duped) ruler. Rosaura is alternately a woman wronged and a warrior in masculine clothes, part man, part woman, as she explains to Segismund while preparing to join his forces. Clotaldo is the prince's committed tutor and only source of human contact, as well as his warden and jail keeper,

at once compassionate and cruel. Clarion, the play's clown figure, or *gracioso,* is simultaneously cowardly buffoon and truth-
telling pragmatist.

This duality of character in *Life Is a Dream* has its structural
counterpart in the many parallels throughout the play, and is em-
blematic of the intricate baroque symmetry uniting the various
elements of plot and subplot. Shortly after it is revealed that
Rosaura has been abandoned by her father, Segismund's aban-
donment comes to light. No sooner has Duke Astolf declared
himself the likely heir to the Polish throne than King Basil an-
nounces his intention to observe the actions of the freed Segismund at court. While Stella for a time is destined to be Astolf's
queen, she ultimately will reign as the wife of the future King
Segismund. Rosaura serves Stella as a lady-in-waiting under the
assumed name of Astrea, which, like her mistress's name, means
"star," a sidereal etymology upon which Segismund expounds at
the close of Act II, scene 7. As Rosaura laments her deception by
Astolf through a false promise of marriage, she recounts the
heartfelt sympathy she received from her own deceived mother.
Clarion shares the fates of two unfortunate masters, wandering
lost with Rosaura through the mountains of Poland and later
suffering imprisonment with Segismund for his knowledge of
court secrets learned while in the prince's service. Locked in a remote tower, Clarion even invites comparison with King Basil's
belief in planetary augury when he attempts to read his fortune
in a deck of cards.

Similarly strange for their grounding in an earlier theatrical
tradition are the lengthy monologues strewn throughout *Life
Is a Dream.* The most extreme are Basil's ponderous first-act
speech of 255 lines and Rosaura's 232-line counterpart in Act
III. Such virtuosic set pieces have been likened to operatic arias,
and are almost always shortened in contemporary performances.
In nearly all cases, they serve a narrative function, and these
expository declamations, typically of background information
and/or events that have transpired offstage, are vestiges of the
unity of time, place, and action first proposed by Aristotle as
conventions for the drama of classical antiquity. To ensure that

a theater piece treats one subject in one location over the course of a single day, many playwrights felt compelled to compress their story lines by making use of speeches in this way. Calderón followed Lope and other early Spanish Renaissance dramatists in flouting these strictures, although *Life Is a Dream* still employs only two basic settings—the mountain prison and the Polish court—as well as more or less unified action (which includes the well-integrated Rosaura/Clotaldo/Astolf subplot) over the course of as little as three days.

Rosaura's disguises, first as a male traveler and then as Astrea, may also seem like forced contrivances to today's theatergoers, yet they mirror the play's central secrets, the final revelations of which lead to a neat resolution of the plot. Rosaura's, Basil's, Clotaldo's, and Astolf's concealments are thematically linked to the poles of fiction/dream and reality/wakefulness proposed by the play, and underscore the inherent tensions between empirical observation and absolutist belief.

Calderón's masterly use of conceptism—witty, allusive conceits couched in rich language—is also characteristic of seventeenth-century Spanish writing, and was a favored stylistic technique of his near-contemporaries Francisco Quevedo and Baltasar Gracián. Such expert touches of formalistic flair are responsible for some of the most memorable poetic passages in *Life Is a Dream,* including the wretched Segismund's prison-cell lament in Act I, scene 2, Astolf's somewhat foppish praise of Stella in Act I, scene 5, and Clarion's magniloquent description of Rosaura's horse as an embodiment of the four elements in Act III, scene 9. (Segismund's starry wooing of Rosaura-as-Astrea mentioned above also falls into this category.) Calderón reveals his virtuosic facility with baroque verse by ending each speech tidily with a summary listing of every element included in the elaborate comparison. This Spanish Golden Age taste for seemingly logical paradox in free linguistic play may also be observed in Segismund's rationale for wishing to strangle Rosaura in Act I, scene 2, and in the latter's long and intricate exchange with Clotaldo on the relative merits of giving versus receiving in Act III, scene 8.

Many of Calderón's plays, *Life Is a Dream* among them, were first performed in *corrales,* outdoor spaces located in large, open courtyards. The configurations of these theaters, along with the limitations of Renaissance stagecraft, virtually dictated certain conventions of Golden Age plays. In seventeenth-century Spain, a theatrical presentation would generally take place in the afternoon, in natural light on a curtainless stage with bare-bones décor. The characters would often refer to setting or locale, as well as to the weather and such pertinent dramatic details as the time of day, as in the first one hundred lines or so of *Life Is a Dream.* Scene changes were frequently signaled simply by actors leaving the stage empty for a short period of time, although on occasion some sort of rudimentary backdrop might be employed. Perhaps most foreign to a modern concept of theater, though, was that plays of this period, even those as serious and well crafted as *Life Is a Dream,* were performed between additional entertainments that likewise affected their theatrical composition. Though by Calderón's day songs with musical accompaniment and the recitation of poetic prologues preceded dramatic functions infrequently, the first act of a Golden Age play was typically followed by an *entremés* or *sainete,* a short comic farce dealing with the lower classes, while a sort of ballet was staged after Acts II and III. Once the action resumed, the audience often found it difficult to remember, over the hours of a long afternoon's bill, what exactly had transpired in the drama, so it was treated to a repetitious summary monologue, which recounted the plot of the previous act or acts. In *Life Is a Dream,* Basil's explanation to Clotaldo at the beginning of Act II, which repeats the reasons why Segismund has been brought to court, is one clear instance of this practical requirement, as is Rosaura's recapitulation of her entire role in the drama in Act III, scene 9. This speech, in fact, is so lengthy that midway through it Rosaura self-consciously suggests, "Let's skip a bit."

Several of Calderón's works were translated during his lifetime, and versions of his plays appeared continually in French, Ital-

ian, Dutch, English, and German productions. Calderón's status as one of Europe's premier dramatists continued until the
end of the eighteenth century, during which period his works
were performed with a frequency second only to Molière's. After hundreds of years of Reformation challenges to Catholic
hegemony on the Continent, and with the rise of an Enlighten-
ment aesthetic that considered Calderón's sensibility too broadly
imaginative and emotive for the rational demands of the neo-
classical temperament, Calderón's standing in Europe suffered
from the prevailing winds of change. In his native land, however,
he remained the most performed playwright until his popularity
was eclipsed by Tirso de Molina during Romanticism's relatively
late flowering in Spain. The somewhat medieval religiosity that
critics point out in many of Calderón's dramas—somber and
retributive—was a stumbling block for a reawakened Europe
just emerging, unlike the more isolated Spain, from the sweep-
ing secular humanism of the Renaissance. During this time,
the most frequent productions of Calderón were of relatively
lesser-known comedies, since the ultimately doctrinaire aura of
Catholicism in many of his tragedies and, of course, the *autos
sacramentales,* placed him effectively off-limits and out of sympathy with northern Protestant audiences.

If Shakespeare owes his present-day standing as the West's
finest playwright to his rescue by and subsequent revival
through the British Romantic establishment, it might be claimed
that Calderón's current status in the canon of Western literature
is due to a similar rediscovery, by the German Romantics. *Life
Is a Dream* was by far the most popular play in Germany for
practically the entire first half of the nineteenth century, and
such influential German poets and critics as A. W. Schlegel,
Friedrich von Schiller, and Johann Wolfgang von Goethe enthu-
siastically hailed a figure they considered to be the most "aristocratic" of playwrights. Calderón's fame at this time was so great
that Percy Bysshe Shelley undertook a partial translation of *El
mágico prodigioso,* while the Spanish master's impact on German sensibilities extended to a host of retranslations and adaptations for the stage (some of these in musical productions).

In an increasingly liberal nineteenth-century Spain, however, Calderón's foothold on the Castilian imagination continued to slip. The progressivism that culminated in the works of the Generation of '98—writers such as Miguel de Unamuno, Pío Baroja, Azorín, and Ramón María del Valle-Inclán, who explored Spain's cultural rebirth following the loss of its last overseas colony—relegated the Golden Age author to the status of a reactionary representative of what had become by that time a rapidly modernizing nation. Nevertheless, in English-speaking countries throughout the twentieth century there was, and continues to be of late, a flurry of translation activity reintroducing Calderón in general and *Life Is a Dream* in particular to everbroadening audiences. In the end, it is safe to assert that *Life Is a Dream* has attained the well-deserved stature of a world classic, perhaps more respected than understood or loved. When it is staged these days, often in American regional theaters, productions predictably emphasize the play's universalizing qualities, and focus considerably less on Spanish period effects. Calderón, however, continues to win over adherents to his unique and impressive oeuvre as he did Shelley, whose effusive, if chauvinistic, remarks in a letter of 1819 reflect an admittedly biased though still commonly voiced sentiment: "I have read about twelve of his plays; some of them certainly deserve to be ranked among the grandest and most perfect productions of the human mind. He exceeds all modern dramatists with the exception of Shakespeare."

Suggestions for Further Reading

Aycock, Wendell M., and Sydney P. Cravens, eds., *Calderón de la Barca at the Tercentenary: Comparative Views,* Lubbock: Texas Tech Press, 1982.

Benabu, Isaac, *Reading for the Stage: Calderón and His Contemporaries,* Woodbridge, Suffolk, UK: Tamesis, 2003.

Bergman, Ted L. L., *The Art of Humour in the Teatro Breve and Comedias of Calderón de la Barca,* Woodbridge, Suffolk, UK: Tamesis, 2003.

Blue, William R., *The Development of Imagery in Calderón's Comedias,* York, S.C.: Spanish Literature Publications Co., 1983.

Bryans, John V., *Calderón de la Barca: Imagery, Rhetoric and Drama,* London: Tamesis, 1977.

Cascardi, Anthony J., *The Limits of Illusion: A Critical Study of Calderón,* Cambridge, UK: Cambridge University Press, 1984.

De Armas, Frederick A., *The Return of Astraea: An Astral-Imperial Myth in Calderón,* Lexington: University Press of Kentucky, 1986.

———, ed., *The Prince in the Tower: Perceptions of* La vida es sueño, Lewisburg, Penn.: Bucknell University Press, 1993.

De Armas, Frederick A., David M. Gitlitz, and José A. Madrigal, eds., *Critical Perspectives on Calderón de la Barca,* Lincoln, Neb.: Society of Spanish and Spanish-American Studies, 1981.

Delgado Morales, Manuel, *The Calderonian Stage: Body and Soul,* Lewisburg, Penn.: Bucknell University Press, 1997.

Edwards, Gwynne, *The Prison and the Labyrinth: Studies in Calderonian Tragedy,* Cardiff: University of Wales Press, 1978.

Fox, Dian, *Kings in Calderón: A Study in Characterization and Political Theory,* London: Tamesis, 1986.

———, *Refiguring the Hero: From Peasant to Noble in Lope de Vega and Calderón,* University Park: Pennsylvania State University Press, 1991.

Greer, Margaret Rich, *The Play of Power: Mythological Court Dramas of Calderón de la Barca,* Princeton, N.J.: Princeton University Press, 1991.

Heigl, Michaela, *Theorizing Gender, Sexuality, and the Body in Calderonian Theatre,* New Orleans: University Press of the South, 2004.

Hesse, Everett W., *Calderón de la Barca,* New York: Twayne Publishers, 1967.

Hildner, David Jonathan, *Reason and the Passions in the Comedias of Calderón,* Philadelphia: J. Benjamins, 1982.

Honig, Edwin, *Calderón and the Seizures of Honor,* Cambridge, Mass.: Harvard University Press, 1972.

Kurtz, Barbara E., *The Play of Allegory in the Autos Sacramentales of Pedro Calderón de la Barca,* Washington, D.C.: Catholic University of America Press, 1991.

Levy, Kurt, Jesús Ara, and Gethin Hughes, eds., *Calderón and the Baroque Tradition,* Waterloo, Ont., Canada: Wilfrid Laurier University Press, 1985.

Maraniss, James E., *On Calderón,* Columbia: University of Missouri Press, 1978.

McGaha, Michael D., ed., *Approaches to the Theater of Calderón,* Washington, D.C.: University Press of America, 1982.

Mujica, Barbara Louise, *Calderón's Characters: An Existential Point of View,* Barcelona: Puvill, 1980.

O'Connor, Thomas Austin, *Myth and Mythology in the Theater of Pedro Calderón de la Barca,* San Antonio, Tex.: Trinity University Press, 1988.

Parker, Alexander A., and Deborah Kong, eds., *The Mind and*

  Art of Calderón: Essays on the Comedias, Cambridge,
  UK: Cambridge University Press, 1988.

Rupp, Stephen James, *Allegories of Kingship: Calderón and the
  Anti-Machiavellian Tradition,* University Park: Pennsylvania
  State University Press, 1996.

Sloman, Albert E., *The Dramatic Craftsmanship of Calderón:
  His Use of Earlier Plays,* Oxford: Dolphin Book Co., 1958.

Sullivan, Henry W., *Calderón in the German Lands and the
  Low Countries: His Reception and Influence, 1654–1980,*
  Cambridge, UK: Cambridge University Press, 1983.

Suscavage, Charlene E., *Calderón: The Imagery of Tragedy,*
  New York: Peter Lang, 1991.

Ter Horst, Robert, *Calderón: The Secular Plays,* Lexington:
  University Press of Kentucky, 1982.

Tyler, Richard W., and Sergio Elizondo, *The Characters, Plots,
  and Settings of Calderón's Comedias,* Lincoln, Neb.: Society
  of Spanish and Spanish-American Studies, 1981.

Wardropper, Bruce W., ed., *Critical Essays on the Theatre of
  Calderón,* New York: New York University Press, 1965.

A Note on the Translation

Some twenty English-language translations of *La vida es sueño* may currently be found. The majority of these have been published in book form, though some remain in manuscript, and many are now out of print. These texts vary considerably in aesthetic conceptualization and poetic strategy, and range from literal prose versions to free-verse renderings to abridged adaptations for the stage. The present translation of Calderón's masterpiece represents the first attempt to render the drama entirely in analogous meter and rhyme since 1853, when both Denis Florence MacCarthy and Edward FitzGerald, with varying degrees of success, contemporaneously produced full-length English-language versions of the play. The earliest translation of *La vida es sueño,* by Malcolm Cowan, dates from 1830.

The language of this translation has attempted to retain a hint of archaism without striving to sound pseudo-Shakespearean. One aim of this approach has been to allow contemporary English-language audiences to eavesdrop, as it were, on the aesthetics of dramatic production in a Spain whose nearly four-hundred-year remove in time is surpassed by a cultural distance vaster still. All Spanish syllabic lines have been converted into English strong-stress meters: that is, the eleven-beat hendecasyllable into iambic pentameter, octosyllables into iambic tetrameter, and so on. Rhyme appears wherever it does in Calderón's original Spanish, while the alternating assonantal rhymes of the extended narrative passages have been turned into quatrains in which the second and fourth lines produce an off-rhyme in English. Since Calderón utilized a variety of metrical and rhyming patterns—*romance, redondillas, silvas, décimas, quintillas,* and *octavas reales*—the reader should readily note all instances of poetic shift in the present English-language play. The somewhat shorter Spanish line has likewise been retained to differentiate Spanish Golden Age metrics from Elizabethan poetics.

No manuscript of *La vida es sueño* survives, and early published versions differ considerably. The present translation follows in almost all cases the text presented by Ciriaco Morón Arroyo in the Cátedra "Letras Hispánicas" series, which maintains the scenic divisions created by Juan Eugenio de Hartzenbusch in his *Biblioteca de autores españoles* of 1851.

Life Is a Dream

Characters

SEGISMUND, *the prince, son of Basil*
BASIL, *King of Poland*
ROSAURA, *a Russian noblewoman*
CLOTALDO, *an old nobleman, father of Rosaura*
ASTOLF, *Duke of Moscow*
STELLA, *niece of King Basil*
CLARION, *a clown*
GUARDS
SERVANTS
SOLDIERS
LADIES-IN-WAITING
COURTIERS
MUSICIANS

The action alternates between a remote mountain prison in Poland and the Polish court, including their environs.

Characters

ACT I

Scene i

[*Enter* ROSAURA, *high on a mountainside in Poland, dressed in a man's traveling clothes. Having been thrown from her horse, she descends while addressing the runaway animal.*]

ROSAURA: Dash off, wild hippogriff!
Why are you charging wind-swift down
  a cliff
So barren and strewn with stone
You'll only tumble headlong all alone
Into its tangled maze?   5
Dull lightning bolt devoid of fiery rays,
Scaled fish, bird shy of hue,
Where is that horse sense instinct
  tendered you?
Dwell on these pinnacles
And be a Phaëthon for the animals,   10
While I, forlorn and blind,
Oblivious to the path fate has in mind
For me, descend the brow
Of this imposing, sun-burnt mountain now
And dodge its tangled hair,   15
Emerging I could hardly tell you where.
This welcome, Poland, would
Be more hospitable if strangers could

        Sign in with ink, not blood.
        I'm hardly here, but bleed hard on your mud.   20
        Still, fortune foresees all:
        Where does one find compassion for a fall?

[*Enter* CLARION, *a clown.*]

CLARION: One? Make that two of us
        And count me in when you kick up a fuss!
        My lady, may I speak?   25
        As two, we left our native land to seek
        Adventure in the world,
        Both saw strange sights, watched miseries
          unfurled
        Before our very eyes
        And tumbled down these hills to great surprise.   30
        I've shared all your duress,
        So tell me now, what's causing you distress?

ROSAURA: I'd hoped to spare your ear
        From my complaining, Clarion, out of fear
        A servant might be prone   35
        To start bemoaning troubles not his own.
        There's so much joy to find
        In sorrows, one philosopher opined,
        That those who've naught to rue
        Will seek a share so they can grumble, too.   40

CLARION: Philosopher? Perhaps
        A whiskered drunk! I say a hundred slaps
        Would leave the rogue well served,
        And then I bet he'd whine they weren't
          deserved!
        But what should we do now,   45
        My lady, stranded here, you will allow,
        At just the worst of times,

                Right when the sun is seeking western
                   climes?

ROSAURA: Who ever tread such singular terrain?
                If my imagination will refrain   50
                From fooling with my sight,
                I dare say, by this day's fainthearted light,
                I see a structure rise
                Amid those peaks.

CLARION: Now, either my heart lies
                Or hope views what it wills.   55

ROSAURA: A palace born within these barren hills
                So rustic and so crude
                The sun is loath to look on frames so rude;
                An edifice of rough
                Construction, fashioned ruggedly enough   60
                That, lying at the base
                Of rocky crags that touch the sun's warm face
                And bask in brilliant lights,
                It looks like some huge stone pitched from
                   the heights.

CLARION: Let's wander down a bit   65
                Where we can get a better look at it.
                If destiny is kind,
                The castle dwellers there might feel inclined
                To take us in.

ROSAURA: Its door
                Stands open like a gaping mouth mid-roar   70
                And night springs from its jowls,
                Engendered in the cavern of its bowels.

[*Chains clank within.*]

CLARION: Good God, do I hear chains?

ROSAURA: I'm frozen stiff, but fire runs through
                my veins!

CLARION: Just dig my early grave!   75
                If that isn't a captive galley slave,
                My fear's deceiving me.

Scene ii

[SEGISMUND, *within.*]

SEGISMUND: Oh, abject wretch! To bear such misery!

ROSAURA: What voice sounds these laments?
                Fresh sorrows and new torments wrack my
                        sense!   80

CLARION: Strange fears besiege my head!

ROSAURA: Come, Clarion.

CLARION: Lady mine!

ROSAURA: It's time we fled
                From this enchanted tower.

CLARION: I hesitate
                To flee our only refuge in this strait.

ROSAURA: Do I glimpse from afar   85
                The weak and pallid gleam as of a star
                Whose feeble, flickering haze,
                The emanation of dull heat and rays,
                Diffuses through some room
                A light so pale it magnifies the gloom?   90

Yes, even standing here
I spy unlighted hollows that appear
To be dark prison cells,
The rank tomb where some live cadaver
    dwells.
How wondrous! There within,   95
A squalid man lies clad in animal skin,
Restrained by chains, it seems,
His only company those sickly beams.
Since we've no hope for flight,
Let's listen as he chronicles the plight   100
Of his lost liberty.

[SEGISMUND *is revealed, chained beneath a faint light and
dressed in animal pelts.*]

SEGISMUND: Oh, abject wretch! To bear such misery!
                I've struggled, heavens, night and morn
                To comprehend what horrid crime
                Was perpetrated at the time   105
                When I, offending you, was born.
                At last I grasp why cosmic scorn
                Should be my portion after birth:
                Your justice may enlist no dearth
                Of reasons to be harsh with me   110
                As being born, I've come to see,
                Is mankind's greatest sin on earth.
                But still I venture, stars, to learn,
                If only for some peace of mind,
                Discounting my dark birth, what kind   115
                Of crime could warrant in return
                A punishment as fierce and stern
                As this I live, a living hell?
                Weren't all the others born as well?
                If all came in the world this way,   120
                What sort of privilege had they
                I'll never savor in this cell?

The bird is born with sumptuous hues
And hatches wielding beauty's power.
In time, this lovely feathered flower,   125
A winged bouquet of shades, will choose
To soar the sky's blue avenues
As swift as anything flies free,
Forsaking the sure sympathy
And peaceful quiet of its nest.   130
As I've more soul within my breast,
Should I enjoy less liberty?
The beast is born, and on its fur
Fair markings leave their bold design.
In time, this horoscope-like sign   135
Drawn by the master picturer
Will learn, when human cravings stir
In cruel self-interest, not to flee
But act as cruel as man can be,
Like some dread monster in a maze.   140
As worthier of higher praise,
Should I enjoy less liberty?
The fish is born not breathing air,
A freak amid sea slime and grass.
In time, this scaly ship will pass   145
Unfettered through the waves, aware
It's free to swim the hydrosphere
And, measuring the watery
Expanses of the open sea,
Conceive of greater spaces still.   150
As I possess the freer will,
Should I enjoy less liberty?
The stream is born, a snake that wends
Its way where wildflowers bide.
In time, this silvery fresh will glide   155
Along green banks as it extends
A song of gratitude that sends
Its thanks up toward the canopy
For granting it the majesty

Of open fields in which to flow.   160
As I've more life within me, though,
Should I enjoy less liberty?
In suffering that's known no ease,
I smolder like Mount Etna, whose
Release comes only when it spews   165
Its heart out of its vortices.
Which edicts, laws, codes, or decrees
Deny a man who's sepulchered
That sweetest privilege proffered,
The natural prerogative   170
Just God above would freely give
To beast and stream, to fish and bird?

ROSAURA: His words evoke in me a fear
And sympathy that cloud my sense.

SEGISMUND: Who's overheard my soul's laments?   175
Clotaldo?

CLARION: Answer, "Yes, I'm here!"

ROSAURA: Alas, none but this mountaineer
Who, stumbling on your cell, now braves
The melancholy it encaves.

[SEGISMUND *seizes her.*]

SEGISMUND: I've no choice but to kill you so   180
You'll never live to know I know
You know how craven I've behaved.
My honor dictates that I stretch
These arms about your neck and wring
The life from you for eavesdropping.   185

CLARION: I'm hard of hearing, and didn't catch
A word you said!

ROSAURA: Were you, poor wretch,
                    Born human, I would surely meet
                    With mercy, prostrate at your feet.

SEGISMUND: Your voice could cause my heart to melt,   190
                    Your presence challenge all I've felt,
                    Your guise make my disquiet complete.
                    Who are you? Pent inside these walls,
                    I've known so little of the world—
                    My cradle and my grave unfurled   195
                    Before me in this tower's palls—
                    That from my birth my mind recalls—
                    If birth it was—no other place
                    Than these backwoods of barren space
                    Where I endure in wretched strife,   200
                    A living skeleton stripped of life,
                    A dead man only live by grace.
                    In all my days, I've spoken to
                    One man and one alone. He knows
                    The grievous nature of my woes   205
                    And taught me all I hold most true
                    About the earth and heavens. You
                    Appear now, shocked that I could be
                    The monstrous human rarity
                    You spy mid ghosts and wraiths,
                        so feast   210
                    Your eyes: I'm a man of a beast
                    And a beast of a man, you'll see.
                    Yet, while I've paid misfortune's price,
                    I've versed myself in politics,
                    Observing how the wild brutes mix   215
                    And listening to the birds' advice.
                    My measurements have been precise
                    When I map starry paths in space.
                    But you alone possess the grace
                    To cause my anger to subside,   220

My eyes to doubt what they've descried,
My ears to trust all they embrace.
And every time I fix my gaze
On you, I feel fresh wonder soar.
The more I look at you, the more   225
I want to see you all my days.
It's dropsy making my eyes glaze
And brim with water now, I think,
For knowing it's sure death to drink,
They drink you in still more like wells.   230
Still, seeing that my seeing spells
My death, I'll die to let them graze.
Oh, let me look on you and die!
For all I know, come my last breath,
If seeing you will mean my death,   235
What will not seeing you imply?
Much worse than death would signify—
Dread fury, rage, and wracking pain.
At least in death my teeming brain
Will grasp life's harsh finality: 240
Why grant life to a wretch like me
When happy mortals can be slain?

ROSAURA: I'm awed by you, yet filled with dread.
Still marveling at your tender speech,
I find it difficult to reach   245
Conclusions that remain unsaid.
I'll only say the heavens led
Me here to this sequestered site
To help console me in my plight,
If by "consoling" what is meant   250
Is happening on a wretch who's pent
And makes one's own distress seem slight.
A learned man down on his luck,
The story goes, became dirt poor
But soon surmised he would endure   255

By feeding on the herbs he'd pluck.
"Who else," he asked, "could be so struck
By worldly cares and yet abide?"
At this, he turned around and spied
His answer straightway, noticing   260
Another wise man gathering
The wild herbs he'd cast aside.
I've sighed my fate could be no worse;
Mere living seemed a daunting task.
So when it came my turn to ask,   265
"Who else could suffer through the curse
Of luck so ill-starred and adverse?"
You answered me with sympathy
Because of which I now can see
How all you've said was but a ploy   270
To turn my sorrows into joy
And thereby ease my pain for me.
So if this sharing of my woes
Can soothe your pain to some extent,
Take all you wish by listening,   275
I'll still possess no end of them.
My name is . . .

Scene iii

[CLOTALDO, *offstage.*]

CLOTALDO: Tower guards! Are you
             Asleep or simply faint of heart?
             Your negligence let travelers
             Gain access to the prison yard!   280

ROSAURA: I don't know what to think or feel!

SEGISMUND: My jail keeper Clotaldo's men!
             When will my sorrows ever end?

[*Offstage.*]

CLOTALDO: Look lively and be vigilant!
             They must be seized, alive or dead!   285
             Be careful now, they may be armed.

[*The sound of guards offstage.*]

             Oh, treason!

CLARION: Tower guards—yes, you
             Who've kindly let us come this far—
             As long as there's a choice involved,
             We're easier to take alive!   290

[*Enter* CLOTALDO *with a pistol, and soldiers, all with their
faces hidden.*]

CLOTALDO: Make sure your faces are concealed
             As this precaution's been devised
             To keep whoever happens by
             From recognizing all of you.

CLARION: I love a jolly masquerade!   295

CLOTALDO: Oh, ignorant, misguided fools!
             By trespassing upon a site
             Off limits to all wayfarers,
             You violate the king's decree
             That stipulates no sojourner   300
             Should ever set his curious eyes
             Upon the wonder mid these crags.
             Surrender and give up your swords
             Or else this firearm, an asp
             Recast in metal molds, will spew   305
             A venom forth that penetrates

SEGISMUND: Say, tyrant master, what you will,
              But do these wanderers no harm.   310
              I'll hold my bleak existence cheap
              And rot here chained among your guards—
              Where, by God's name, I'm left no choice
              But to dismember this bound flesh
              With my own hands or teeth—before   315
              I'll stand for their unhappiness
              Or end up, mid these lonely crests,
              Lamenting more of your abuse.

CLOTALDO: If, Segismund, you know full well
              How large your own misfortunes loom,   320
              Enough for heaven to have sealed
              Your doom before your birth; if you
              Know that this prison serves to keep
              In check your haughty fits of rage,
              A bridle for your furious starts   325
              To harness them in lieu of reins,
              Why must you go on raving? Guards,
              Make fast these prison doors and keep
              This man again from sight.

[*They bolt the door.* SEGISMUND's *voice is heard within.*]

SEGISMUND: How right
              You've been, cruel skies, to wrest from me   330
              My liberty! I'd only rise
              Against you like a giant who,
              To smash the crystallinity
              The sun displays upon its route,
              Would pile jasper mountains high   335
              Atop a base of solid stone.

CLOTALDO: Perhaps, preventing such an act
              Explains why you must suffer so.

Scene iv

ROSAURA: As I've observed how arrogance
              Offends your grave propriety,   340
              It would be senseless not to beg
              You for this life prone at your feet.
              May you be moved to pity me
              And be not unrelenting should
              Humility or arrogance   345
              Make sympathy impossible.

CLARION: Humility or Arrogance
              Should work. As stock protagonists
              They move the plots bad playwrights use
              In far too many sacred skits.   350
              But if they don't, then mid extremes,
              Not overhumble or too proud,
              I beg you, somewhere in between,
              Do what you can to help us out!

CLOTALDO: Guards! Guards!

SOLDIERS: My lord!

CLOTALDO: Disarm these two   355
              And blindfold them at once! These men
              Must never be allowed to leave
              These confines or retrace their steps.

ROSAURA: My sword, sir. Duty and respect
              Oblige me to surrender this   360
              To you alone, the principal

Among us here, and not permit
Its cession to a lesser power.

CLARION: My own is such the worse for wear
That anyone could take it. Here.   365

ROSAURA: I yield it, should I not be spared,
To mark the pity I've been shown,
A token worthy of regard
Because of one who wore it girt
In days gone by. Indulge my charge   370
And hold it dear, for I know not
What muted secret it enfolds,
Except to say this gilded sword
Contains great mysteries untold
And, having sworn on it a pledge,   375
Am come to Poland to avenge
A grave wrong done me.

CLOTALDO: Stars above!
Can this be? All my old suspense
And sorrow, my remorse and grief
Conspire to cause me still more pain.   380
Who gave you this?

ROSAURA: A woman did.

CLOTALDO: How was the lady called?

ROSAURA: Her name
May not be spoken.

CLOTALDO: Is this your
Assumption or do you avow
That there's some secret in this sword?   385

ROSAURA: She who bestowed it said, "Set out
                  For Poland, using all the charm
                  And artful cunning you possess
                  To make the noblemen you meet
                  Bear witness to this testament.   390
                  I'm certain one among them there
                  Will show you favor in your quest,"
                  Though she declined to give his name
                  In case the man she meant was dead.

CLOTALDO: God help me! What assails my ears?   395
                  Now, how will I contrive to prove
                  That what has just transpired here
                  Is no illusion, but the truth?
                  This is the sword I left behind
                  With fair Viola as a pledge   400
                  That whosoever wore it girt
                  Upon his thigh within my ken
                  Would find himself a much-loved son
                  And me a sympathetic sire.
                  But now, alas, what can I do?   405
                  Chaotic thoughts run through my mind
                  For he who brings this sword in grace
                  Brings with it unawares his death,
                  Condemned before he ever fell
                  On bended knee. This senselessness   410
                  Confounds me! What a ruinous fate
                  And tragic destiny are mine!
                  This is my son; all markers point
                  To these corroborating signs
                  Within my heart, now pulsing at   415
                  The portals of my breast. Its wings
                  Still flutter there, incapable
                  Of forcing back the bolts, akin
                  To one who's locked inside a room
                  And, hearing noises in the street,   420

Peers through a window eagerly.
Like him, my heart cannot conceive
What's happening and, mid such noise,
Looks through the eyes to catch a view,
As eyes are windows of the soul   425
Where hearts pour out in teary dews.
What choice have I? God help me now!
What choice have I? To lead this man
Before the king—how harsh the blow!—
Would mean his certain death. I can't   430
Conceal him, though, and thus infringe
Upon my sworn obedience.
I'm torn between these deeply felt
Emotions and the duteousness
I owe my liege. Why vacillate?   435
Pledged loyalty, and not our lives
Or loves, must needs take precedence.
Just so, let loyalty abide!
I seem now to recall a claim
He made of having solely come   440
To right a wrong, yet well I know
How wronged men can be villainous.
He's not my son, he's not my son!
He does not share my noble blood!
But if some threat to his good name   445
Indeed occurred—a plight no one
Escapes, as honor is composed
Of such infirm material
The slightest touch can shred its weft
And whispered rumor stain its woof—   450
What else would any nobleman
Essay for honor's sake, what else
But seek the satisfaction owed,
However plenteous the peril?
He is my son! He shares my blood!   455
We've witnessed his courageous mien
And as I stand here, wracked with doubt,

One saving recourse comes to me:
I'll go myself to tell the king
That he's my son, but must be killed.   460
If honorable piety
Won't stay his hand, then nothing will.
Now, should I warrant him his life,
I'll join his quest to seek amends
For wrongs endured. But if the king   465
Is overly intransigent
And puts my son to death, he'll die
Not ever knowing I'm his sire.
Come, strangers, we're to journey now,
But rest assured that I'll provide   470
Good company in misery
For, mired in our present doubts,
Unsure which here will live or die,
Whose wretchedness is paramount?

[*Exit all.*]

Scene v

[*Enter* ASTOLF, *escorted by soldiers, and* STELLA, *accompanied by ladies-in-waiting. Music is playing.*]

ASTOLF: Bedazzled by the shimmering rays   475
               Your eyes shoot forth like comet tails,
               The drums and trumpets fire off praise
               In salvos seldom heard in vales,
               Where birds and brooks trill other lays.
               This equal musical delight,   480
               Performed by instruments in thrall
               To one so heavenly a sight,
               Lets feathered clarions sound their call
               And metal birds put notes to flight.
               Their strains, fair lady, honor you   485
               Like cannonades salute the queen,

The birds Aurora's rosy hue,
The trumpets Pallas the Athene,
The flowers Flora damp with dew.
You've banished black night's sunlessness   490
By making light of day, for you're
Aurora, this earth's happiness,
Its Flora, peace, its Pallas, war,
And my heart's queen in loveliness.

STELLA: Such honeyed discourse flows sincere   495
And in accord with how men act,
But one mistake you make, I fear,
Is that fine words can't counteract
A soldier's garb and martial gear.
These militate against you while   500
My being fights your aspect so
Intensely I can't reconcile
The flattery I'm hearing flow
With all the rigor of your style.
For it is vile and indiscreet,   505
Unworthy of the basest brute,
The seed of treachery and deceit,
To trade on wiles to win one's suit
Or guile to speed a maid's defeat.

ASTOLF: You misconstrue my plain intent   510
In voicing all this errant doubt
Concerning what these words have meant.
Here, Stella, with your kind consent,
Is what this cause has been about:
The death of King Eustorge the Third,   515
Proud Poland's monarch, left his son
Prince Basil sovereign afterward.
One sister was my mother, one
Yours. Not to bore you with absurd
Recitals of each king and queen,   520
I'll make this brief. Fair Clorilene,

Your mother—and to me, Her Grace,
Who now rules in a better place
Beneath the starry damascene—
Was elder, with no progeny   525
But you. Her younger sister was
Your aunt, but mother unto me,
Fair Recisunda, whom God does
Hold likewise dear in memory.
In Moscow, where I came of age,   530
She'd married. Here, I must forgo
Strict sequence and turn back a page:
King Basil, lady, as you know,
Has lost the war all mortals wage
Against Time. Ever with a mind   535
To study, he was disinclined
To woo. His childless queen now dead,
Our bloodlines stand us in good stead
To be the heirs he'll leave behind.
You hold a strong claim to the throne—   540
His elder sister's daughter would—
But I, a male, the fully grown
Son of his younger sister, should
Be favored to ascend alone.
We sought our uncle, then, impelled   545
To plead the justness of each case.
His reconciling us compelled
The naming of this time and place
So that our meeting could be held.
Such was my aim in setting out   550
From Moscow's distant, lovely land.
I've come for Poland's crown without
A fight, but found this fight on hand,
Though I've declined to press the bout.
Oh, may the people, God of Love,   555
Precise astrologers they are,
Be wise like you and think well of
Our union! Let them thank the star

That designates you queen above,
For you're the queen I choose! Be shown   560
The honors you deserve! So please
It that our uncle yield his throne,
Your virtue bring you victories
And my love make this realm your own.

STELLA: I trust my own heart shares the aim   565
               You've set forth in your dashing speech.
               I only wish that I could claim
               The throne now sits within my reach
               So you could rule with lasting fame.
               Still, I confess you must convince   570
               Me that your faith will pass the test
               Of quelling my suspicions since
               The portrait pendant on your chest
               Belies these fine words from a . . . prince.

ASTOLF: I'd hoped to give you a complete   575
               Account of this, but know not how
               As trumpets noisily entreat
               Attendance on the king, who now
               Approaches with his royal suite.

Scene vi

[*Trumpets blare. Enter the aged King* BASIL *with retinue.*]

STELLA: Wise Thales!

ASTOLF: Learned Euclid, hail!   580

STELLA: You rule today . . .

ASTOLF: Today you dwell . . .

STELLA: Mid starry signs . . .

ASTOLF: Mid starry trail . . .

STELLA: And calculate . . .

ASTOLF: And measure well . . .

STELLA: Each orbit's path . . .

ASTOLF: Each sphere's true scale.

STELLA: Oh, let me twirl like ivy round . . .   585

ASTOLF: Oh, let me lie down duty bound . . .

STELLA: Your trunk, as fitting and discreet.

ASTOLF: Here prostrate at your royal feet.

BASIL: Dear niece and nephew, our profound
                   Embrace! As loyal from the start   590
                   To our most sentimental plans,
                   You come with such a show of heart
                   That we pronounce you, by these banns,
                   True equals, each a part to part.
                   We ask, though, since our person nears   595
                   Exhaustion from the weight of years,
                   That you respectfully refrain
                   From speaking, as it will be plain
                   Our speech will soon amaze your ears.
                   For well you know—now mind our words,   600
                   Beloved nephew, dearest niece,
                   Grand nobles of the Polish court,
                   Good subjects, kin, friends we esteem—
                   For well you know, men have bestowed
                   On us the epithet of "wise"   605
                   To honor our enlightenment.
                   Against Oblivion and Time,

Timanthes in his portraits and
Lysippus in his sculptures grand
Proclaim us "Basil Rex, the Great"   610
And so we're called throughout these lands.
For well you know, the sciences
Are what we've loved and cherished most,
Fine mathematic formulae
By which we've robbed Time of its role,   615
Foreseeing what the future holds,
The only source of its renown,
And presaged more events each day.
For when our charts reveal accounts
Of incidents set to occur   620
In centuries still unbegun,
The dupe is dull chronology
As we glimpse first what's yet to come.
Those circular, snow-colored spheres
In glassy canopies that move   625
Illuminated by the sun
But rent by cycles of the moon;
Those gleaming, diamantine orbs
And planets crystalline in space
Where incandescent stars shine bright   630
And zodiacal creatures graze,
Remain the major inquiry
Of our declining years, the books
In which the heavens list all fates,
Benign or far less merciful,   635
On paper strewn with diamond dust
In sapphire ledgers finely lined
With patterned bars of glittering gold,
Inscribed with multitudes of signs.
We study these celestial tomes   640
And let our spirit wander free
In fast pursuit of starry trails
Wherever their swift paths should lead.
Wise heavens, if you'd only stopped

This active mind before it filled   645
Their margins with its commentaries
Or indexed every page at will!
If only you'd conceived our life
As but the first of casualties
Exacted by their wrath, this might   650
Have been our only tragedy.
But those who are misfortune-prone
Feel merit slice them like a knife,
For whomsoever knowledge harms
Is nothing but a suicide!   655
Though we be late in voicing this,
Events tell better tales than speech
And so, to leave this congress awed,
We ask again that you not speak.
Our late wife, your Queen Clorilene,   660
Bore us a male child so ill-starred
The wary skies announced his birth
With wonders patently bizarre.
Before her womb, that sepulcher
Predating life, gave living light   665
Unto the boy—for being born
And dying are indeed alike—
His mother had seen countless times,
Amid the strange delirium
Of dream, a monstrous form not quite   670
A human, but resembling one,
Which disemboweled her from within.
Once covered with her body's blood,
The brute would kill her, then emerge
Half mortal man, half viper slough.   675
Now, come the day the child was born,
These omens proved to be correct,
For dire portents never lie
And strictly see how things will end.
Spheres inauspiciously aligned   680
Provoked the scarlet-blooded sun

To challenge the cold moon to duel
And turned the heavens rubicund.
With all the earth their battleground,
These two celestial lanterns gleamed   685
In savage combat perched on high,
Both beaming bright as they could beam.
The longest and most horrible
Eclipse that ever did transpire—
Besides the one that dimmed the globe   690
The day Our Lord was crucified—
Occurred next. As the planet sensed
Itself engulfed in living flames,
It must have thought the throes of death
Were making its foundations shake.   695
Then, suddenly, the skies grew black
And sturdy buildings lurched and spun.
The clouds rained stones upon the land
And rivers coursed along like blood.
This fatal confluence of stars   700
Or planetary pull prevailed
At Segismund's birth, presaging
The foulness of his soul that day.
For life, he gave his mother death,
And by such savagery affirmed: 705
"I am a man who will not cease
To menace all mankind in turn."
Recurring to the sciences
For guidance, we divined dire plans
For Segismund. We learned our heir   710
Would be the most rebellious man
The world could know, the cruelest prince
And even most ungodly king
Whose reckless rule would leave the realm
Divided and in open rift,   715
A fractious School for Treachery
And roiled Academy of Vice.
These signs revealed one so possessed

Of furious rage and violent crime
We even saw him set his heels   720
Upon us as we lay beneath—
This gives us great distress to say—
The brute soles of his conquering feet!
The silver hairs that grace this crown
Were but a carpet for his steps.   725
Who'd not put credence in such doom
Precisely when such doom is read
Secure in one's own study where
Self-interest plies its influence?
So, putting credence in the fates   730
As prophets given to dispense
Bleak auguries of promised harm
Through omens and foretokened signs,
We ordered that the newborn brute
Be everlastingly confined   735
To find out whether an old sage
Might thwart the dictates of the stars.
The false news of his stillborn birth
Was propagated near and far
While we, forewarned, ordained a tower   740
Be built between the craggy peaks
Of two remote, secluded hills
Where light could scarcely hope to reach
So that these rustic obelisks
Might seal off entry to the place.   745
The strict laws and harsh penalties
For breaking them were then displayed,
Declaring a forbidden zone
Off limits to all sojourners
Who'd think to pass, the grave result   750
Of these events we've just referred.
There Segismund, our son, dwells yet,
Imprisoned, wretched, and forlorn,
Attended by Clotaldo, still
His only company of sorts,   755

Who tutored him in sciences
And catechized him in beliefs
Of Christian faith, the only man
Who's seen him in captivity.
Three issues guide us here: the first,   760
As we hold Poland in such high
Esteem, our lasting wish has been
To free her from the heinous plight
Of serving tyrant kings. Indeed,
A sovereign who would so imperil   765
The native soil that is his realm
Cannot be said to govern well.
The second bears upon the charge
That, by our actions, we've removed
The right to reign from its true line—   770
Of which no codex would approve—
Through lack of Christian charity
As no existing law permits
A man who'd keep another man
From tyranny and insolence   775
To take on those same qualities.
For if our son's a tyrant, then
How may we perpetrate vile crimes
To keep him from committing them?
The third and final point entails   780
Determining to what extent
A person errs too readily
By trusting in foretold events,
For though our heir may be disposed
To outbursts and impetuous acts,   785
This bent is but a tendency.
The direst fate, we know for fact,
Much like the rashest temperament
Or strongest planetary pull,
May boast some influence on free will   790
But cannot make man bad or good.
Engrossed, then, in these quandaries

And hesitant with self-debate,
We hit upon a remedy
That's sure to leave your senses dazed. 795
Tomorrow, we will have enthroned—
Without him knowing he's our son
Or your next king—the man who bears
The fateful name of Segismund.
Beneath our royal canopy 800
And seated in our august place,
He'll have his chance to reign at last
As all our subjects congregate
To pledge their humble fealty.
In doing so, it is our hope 805
To solve three matters that relate
To questions you have heard us pose.
One, should our heir display a mien
Deemed prudent, temperate, and benign
And thus belie what heartless fate 810
Forebode in all it prophesied,
The realm will see its natural line
Restored, as till this hour the prince
Has held court only in those hills,
A neighbor but to woodland things. 815
Two, should our son reveal himself
Rebellious, reckless, arrogant
And cruel, inclined to give free rein
To vice that typifies his bent,
We will have acted piously, 820
Complicit with time-honored codes,
And shine like an unvanquished king
When we depose him from our throne,
Returning him to prison not
In cruelty, but punishment. 825
Three, should the heir apparent
Show the qualities that we suspect,
Our love for Poland's subjects will
Provide you with a king and queen

More worthy of this sceptered crown,   830
To wit, our nephew and our niece.
The individual right to reign
Comes wedded in these two, conferred
By dint of their intended bond,
And both will have what both deserve.   835
For this is our command as king;
The nation's father bids it so.
We urge it as a learned sage;
This wise old man is thus disposed.
If Spanish Seneca believed   840
The king is but a humble slave
Within his own republic's land,
Then we beseech you as the same.

ASTOLF: If, as the man whose future gains
Are most affected by these plans,   845
I have your leave to answer first,
I'll speak for all the court at hand
And say, let Segismund appear!
It's quite sufficient he's your son.

ALL: Restore the royal line! Yes, let   850
Our long-lost prince rule over us!

BASIL: Good subjects, our sincerest thanks
For this outpouring of support.
Escort our kingdom's Atlases
To their respective chamber doors.   855
You'll have your prince upon the morn.

ALL: Long live our great King Basil! Hail!

[*All exit except* BASIL, *who is detained by the entrance of*
CLOTALDO, ROSAURA, *and* CLARION.]

Scene vii

CLOTALDO: A word with you, sire?

BASIL: Our good friend
              Clotaldo! Welcome here today.

CLOTALDO: I might, indeed, have been most pleased   860
              To come, sire, at some other time
              But now it seems a tragic turn
              Must for the moment override
              The privilege our law confers
              And courtesy our ways demand.   865

BASIL: What's happened?

CLOTALDO: A calamity
              That in another circumstance
              Might not have proved so dire a blow
              But been a cause for jubilance.

BASIL: Go on.

CLOTALDO: This handsome youth you see,   870
              Through derring-do or recklessness,
              Gained entrance to the tower grounds
              And saw the prince there pent in chains.
              He is . . .

BASIL: Clotaldo, have no fear.
              Had this occurred some other day,   875
              He would have felt our royal wrath,
              But as we've just divulged this news,
              It matters little that he knows,
              As we've today confirmed the truth.
              Come see us by and by. We've such   880

          A many wonders to relate
          And you so much to do for us.
          You'll learn soon of the role you'll play
          In carrying out the most sublime
          Event this world has countenanced.   885
          As for these prisoners—we're loath
          To punish you for negligence
          And thus, with mercy, pardon them.

[*Exit* BASIL.]

CLOTALDO: Oh, may you rule a thousand years!

Scene viii

CLOTALDO: The heavens have restored my luck!   890
          I've no need for professing here
          That he's my son, as he's been spared.
          Strange pilgrims, seek your wonted route,
          You're free to go.

ROSAURA: I kiss your feet
          A thousand times.

CLARION: I'll . . . *miss* them, too.   895
          So what's one letter more or less
          Between friends who have come to terms?

ROSAURA: You've given me my life back, sire;
          It's thanks to you I walk this earth.
          Consider me eternally   900
          Your grateful slave.

CLOTALDO: A life is more
          Than I can give you in your plight.
          No gentleman that's nobly born

Can live as long as he's aggrieved.
For if it's certain that you come,   905
According to your very words,
To right a wrong that you've been done,
I can't have given your life back;
You didn't have one when you came.
A life defamed is not a life.
  [*Aside.*]
I hope my words leave him inflamed!   910

ROSAURA: I don't possess one, I confess,
Though I accept what you've bestowed
And, after I'm avenged, I'll boast
True honor so pristine and whole   915
The life I claim as mine that day
Will turn aside all future threats
And seem the gift it is at last.

CLOTALDO: Take back this burnished blade you've
    pledged
To bear. I realize your revenge   920
Won't be complete until it shines
Bright with your adversary's blood.
Of course, a sword I once called mine—
I mean, just as I held it now,
Possessing it to some extent—   925
Would know how to avenge.

ROSAURA: I wear
It in your name and once again
Do swear on it I'll be avenged
Despite my able enemy's
Superior force.

CLOTALDO: Is it so great?   930

ROSAURA: So great I must forswear my speech
                And not because I feel I can't
                Confide in you far greater things
                But so you'll not withdraw from me
                The sympathetic ministering   935
                You've shown.

CLOTALDO: I'd sooner join your cause
                If you would but disclose his name.
                This knowledge also might forestall
                My rendering him unmindful aid.
                    [*Aside.*]
                Who is this mortal enemy?   940

ROSAURA: Good sir, so you'll not think I hold
                Our newfound trust in low esteem,
                Know that my honor's bitter foe
                Is no one less than Astolf, Duke
                Of Moscow.

CLOTALDO: [*Aside.*] What a stunning blow   945
                To all these plans! His cause appears
                More grave than even I'd supposed.
                I'll delve more deeply into this.
                If you were born a Muscovite,
                Then he who is your natural lord   950
                Could hardly be accused of
                    slights.
                Return to your ancestral land
                And try to quell this ardent zeal
                That hurls you madly forth.

ROSAURA: The wrong,
                My lord, that left me so aggrieved   955
                Was anything but slight.

CLOTALDO: Perhaps,
                        A slighting slap that stung too hard,
                        Offending—heavens!—that dear cheek?

ROSAURA: The injury was worse by far.

CLOTALDO: What was it, then? I've seen so much   960
                        Of late it scarce could cause alarm.

ROSAURA: I'll tell you, though I know not how,
                        Considering the deep respect
                        And veneration that I feel
                        For you and all this represents.   965
                        How can I venture to explain
                        The riddle these deceptive clothes
                        Conceal? They don't belong to whom
                        You'd guess. Judge wisely what this shows:
                        I'm not who I appear to be   970
                        While Astolf's plan has been to come
                        Wed Stella. Think, how might I feel
                        Insulted? Now I've said too much!

            [*Exit* ROSAURA *and* CLARION.]

CLOTALDO: Beware! Pay heed! Keep up your guard!
                        This is a puzzling labyrinth   975
                        Where even reason toils to find
                        The thread laid down to exit it.
                        My honor is the one aggrieved,
                        Its foe by all accounts quite strong,
                        A vassal I, a woman she.   980
                        May heaven steer my hand from wrongs,
                        Though I'm not certain that it can.
                        The world is one confused abyss;
                        The skies above portend no good
                        And all God's earth seems curious.   985

ACT II

Scene i

[*Enter King* BASIL *and* CLOTALDO.]

CLOTALDO: Your orders have been carried out
              With due dispatch.

BASIL: Then he is come,
              Clotaldo? Tell us what transpired.

CLOTALDO: Sire, this is how the deed was done:
              I plied him with the calming drink   990
              You wished distilled, a most superb
              Confection of ingredients
              That blent the might of sundry herbs.
              The tyrant strength of such a mix,
              Its secret potency concealed,   995
              Deprives a man outright of sense
              And robs him of the power of speech
              While rendering him a living corpse.
              The violence of its attributes
              So dulls the mind and saps the force   1000
              That those benumbed by it lie mute.
              Stale arguments repeatedly
              Ask whether this is possible,
              But time-honored experience
              With scientific principles   1005

Has shown this ever to be true.
For Nature's secrets find a home
In Medicine and there exists
No single creature, plant, or stone
That cannot boast of properties   1010
Unique to it. If base intent
First prompted man to catalogue
The thousand poisons causing death,
How little more had he to search
When classifying qualities   1015
Of every venom known to kill
To find those that would bring on sleep?
Let's lay aside, then, any doubts
Concerning whether this be true,
As reason backed by evidence   1020
Provides us with conclusive proof.
So, bearing that peculiar brew
Of opium and henbane held
Together by the poppy's charms,
I slipped down to the narrow cell   1025
Where Segismund dwelt. There, we spoke
A while of the philosophies
And disciplines he'd mastered, each
From voiceless Nature when she speaks
In mute guise of the hills and skies,   1030
For years at so divine a school
Had trained him in the rhetoric
Of every bird and beast he knew.
Attempting, then, to animate
His spirit and to sound his mind   1035
Before the task at hand, I turned
The topic to the speedy flight
A mighty eagle flaunted high
Above us, scornful of the wind's
Low-lying sphere and soaring like   1040
Some feathery bolt amid the rings
Of fire in the canopy,

A comet blazing on the heights.
I praised the creature's lofty sweep
By saying, "Now I see how right   1045
You are, grand queen who rules all birds,
To feel that you outshine the rest."
Well, that one reference in my speech
To majesty caused such duress
In him, he gave vent to bold thoughts,   1050
His pride and self-conceit stirred up.
The pure blood coursing through his veins
Incites and instigates him thus
To eye great feats, and he exclaimed:
"Then even from the raucous realm   1055
Of birds a leader must emerge
To claim the fealty he compels!
My lessons in misfortune should
Console me with the argument
That only the superior strength   1060
Of jailors keeps my spirits pent,
For I would never willingly
Submit to any mortal's law."
Thus, seeing him enraged by talk
On subjects that recalled the cause   1065
Of so much pain, I offered him
The potent brew. No sooner had
This potion passed from cup to lip
Than all his willful rage collapsed
In heavy sleep. An icy sweat   1070
Coursed through his veins, and every limb
Perspired to such macabre effect
That had I not been warned that this
Was no true death, I would have thought
He'd breathed his last. At just this time,   1075
The men you'd charged to carry out
This bold experiment arrived
And, placing him inside a coach,
Conveyed him to your chambers where

Accommodations following   1080
Strict protocol had been prepared
To lodge him with due majesty.
They laid him sleeping in your bed
And, when the potion's numbing force
Wears off and his deep slumber ends,   1085
They'll serve him as you've ordered, sire,
As if he were the king himself.
So should my fast obeisance
Incline you to reward me well
For all these efforts, lord, my sole   1090
Wish is to learn a puzzling truth.
Pray, pardon me this liberty:
What purpose lies behind this move
Of Segismund unto the court?

BASIL: Clotaldo, well might you voice doubts   1095
About our plan, and these we will
Allay if you'll but hear us out:
As Segismund, our only son,
Was born beneath a baleful star
That, well you know, predestined him   1100
To sorrows, tragedy, and harm,
We'd hoped to probe the heavens now,
As they're incapable of lies
And never ceased revealing signs
Of what that cruelty may be like   1105
Still lodged within his brutal soul.
We'll fathom, then, if stars reprieve
Their harshest edicts or, when moved
By man's restraint and bravery,
Reverse dire omens, for we know   1110
Each person rules his stars and fate.
As this is what we wish to probe,
We've had him brought inside these gates
To tell him he's our son and put
His inclinations to the test,   1115

For should he prove magnanimous,
He'll reign. But if his temperament
Should rage tyrannical and cruel,
He'll be constrained forthwith by chains.
Why is it, you do well to ask,   1120
That this experiment you aid
Could only have been brought to pass
Once deathlike sleep had been induced?
Our sole wish is to satisfy
Your every query with the truth.   1125
Should our son learn he's prince today
But on the morrow come to see
His strange existence once again
Subjected to jail's miseries,
Mere contemplation of this state   1130
Would doubtless lead him to despair,
For once he's found out who he is,
What could console him in his pain?
It's therefore been our plan to leave
The door to pretext open wide   1135
So we may claim that all he saw
Was dreamt, and thereby expedite
Determining two separate things:
His natural condition first,
According to which he'll proceed   1140
To bare his soul in deeds and words,
And second, whether such a ruse
Can furnish solace to a wretch
Who, presently obeyed by all,
Might soon return to prison depths   1145
To understand that he had dreamt.
This he'd do wisely to believe
Because, Clotaldo, in this world
All think they live who only dream.

CLOTALDO: How readily could I present   1150
               Sound refutations of this plan!

But these would serve no purpose now
As I am led to understand
The prince has wakened from his sleep
And, fully conscious, comes this way.   1155

BASIL: Our thought is to withdraw from sight
While you, as tutor, extricate
Your pupil from what lingering doubt
And puzzlement still plague his mind.
The prince will learn the truth at last.   1160

CLOTALDO: Then I have your permission, sire,
To make the plot known?

BASIL: Tell him all.
Thus any danger he may pose
To us while fully cognizant
Will be more easily controlled.   1165

[*Exit* BASIL. *Enter* CLARION.]

Scene ii

CLARION: A halberdier whose reddish hair
And whiskers matched his uniform
Just whacked me good and hard four times
As I ran here to stay informed
Of court events as they unfold.   1170
What window offers finer views—
Not counting those in front-row seats
That ticket vendors hold for you—
Than man's own eyeballs in his head?
For, with or without sense or cent,   1175
Whenever there's a show to see,
He'll sneak a peek with impudence.

CLOTALDO: Ah, faithful Clarion, servant once
To she—sweet heavens!—she indeed
Who, trading in misfortune, brought   1180
To Poland my past infamy.
Good Clarion, have you news?

CLARION: Word is,
My lord, that your benevolence
In stating this intent to right
Rosaura's wrong has her convinced   1185
She should again wear ladies' clothes.

CLOTALDO: It's for the best, lest she be deemed
Too frivolous.

CLARION: Word is, she's changed
Her name to boot and, cleverly
Rechristening herself your niece,   1190
Has watched her reputation surge
At palace, where she now resides,
Attendant to the singular
Dame Stella.

CLOTALDO: Then, I've helped the child
Gain part of her lost honor back.   1195

CLARION: Word is, she's biding time until
The moment your avenging wrath
Restores her honored name in full.

CLOTALDO: No surer thing to bide exists,
For only Time as it transpires   1200
Can put an end to all of this.

CLARION: And word is, too, that she's regaled
With treatment fit a queen at court
By falsely posing as your niece

While I, who served her night and morn,   1205
Am left to die from hunger's want,
Forgotten and ignored by all,
Although a Clarion nonetheless.
For if I ever did sound off
To Astolf, Stella, or the king,   1210
They might be shocked by what they heard.
Both manservants and clarions toot
Like trumpets in this noisy world
And just don't harbor secrets well.
The moment that her fingers lift   1215
This veil of silence from my lips
The song I sing might well be this:
No clarion blaring at first light
Did ever sound more right.

CLOTALDO: Your grievance is well taken, man,   1220
                 But I can help address this plaint.
                 For now, attend me in her stead.

CLARION: Look! Segismund, and unrestrained!

Scene iii

[Enter musicians, singing, and servants attiring SEGISMUND,
who appears dazed.]

SEGISMUND: God save me! What's this I perceive?
                 God help me grasp what I've seen here!   1225
                 I'm awed and not untouched by fear
                 But can't be sure what to believe.
                 Do I stand at the court today
                 Mid sumptuous fabrics, lush brocades,
                 Lithe footmen and fair chambermaids   1230
                 Who serve me in their fine array?
                 Did I awake completely free

And resting in some stately bed
Surrounded, like one highly bred,
With valets to attire me?   1235
To claim I dream would be a ruse,
For sleep and waking aren't the same.
Still, isn't Segismund my name?
Fair heavens, won't you disabuse
My fancy's flight and make it clear   1240
What wondrous circumstances might
Have troubled it thus in the night
To leave me so convinced I'm here?
Whatever turns out to be true,
Who could dispute what I've observed?   1245
I'll let myself be richly served
Here, come what may, in this milieu.

2ND SERVANT: Despondence sits upon his cheek.

1ST SERVANT: Could anyone who's led a life
So drear not bear such signs of strife?   1250

CLARION: Yes, me.

2ND SERVANT: Approach the man and speak.

1ST SERVANT: Another round of singing?

SEGISMUND: Why,
Not now. I don't care to hear more.

2ND SERVANT: You looked so lost and dazed before,
I thought songs might amuse you.

SEGISMUND: My   1255
Ordeal would be as burdensome
Without these choruses of cheer.

I only truly wish to hear
The martial strains of fife and drum.

CLOTALDO: Your Royal Highness! Majesty!   1260
              Oh, let me be the first to kiss
              Your hand lest I appear remiss
              In pledging you my fealty.

SEGISMUND: Is this Clotaldo, my jail keep,
              Whose torments I could once expect,   1265
              Now treating me with such respect?
              I know not if I wake or sleep!

CLOTALDO: The great confusion that you find
              This new condition brings about
              Has raised in you some lingering doubt   1270
              That clouds your reason and your mind.
              I've come to help you be less prone
              To things that cause undue concern
              Because today my lord will learn
              He's heir apparent to the throne   1275
              Of Poland. If till now you've dwelt
              Sequestered vilely far afield,
              It's all because your fate was sealed
              By cards intemperate fate had dealt,
              Portending bane that would allow   1280
              Our empire here to come to grief
              The moment that the laurel leaf
              Would come to grace your august brow.
              But trusting in your better will
              To prove the stars erroneous—   1285
              For men who are magnanimous
              Find ways to overrule them still—
              They've brought you to the palace from
              The tower where they kept your cell,
              Your senses dulled by sleep's deep spell   1290

And all your forces rendered numb.
The king, your sire and my liege lord,
Will come soon, Segismund, to call,
At which time he will tell you all.

SEGISMUND: Vile traitor, born to be abhorred!   1295
What could remain for me to know
When knowing my identity
From this day forward leaves me free
To flaunt my power and cause men woe?
How could you bring this treasonous act   1300
Against your land, to jail your prince
And strip him of all honors, since
No right or reason could retract
A crown, blood pledged?

CLOTALDO: Is this my plight?

SEGISMUND: You've long betrayed our country's laws,   1305
Fawned on the king to aid your cause
And treated me with cruel delight.
For this, the king, the law, and I,
In light of crimes we three condemn,
Now sentence you to die for them   1310
At my own hands.

2ND SERVANT: My lord!

SEGISMUND: Don't try
To thwart me or impede my plan;
I won't be hindered. By the cross,
Dare step between us and I'll toss
You headfirst through that window, man!   1315

1ST SERVANT: Clotaldo, flee!

CLOTALDO: Oblivious dunce,
               To manifest such reckless pride
               Not conscious you've dreamt all you spied!

[*Exit* CLOTALDO.]

2ND SERVANT: Be mindful that . . .

SEGISMUND: Leave here at once!

2ND SERVANT: He looked but to obey his king.   1320

SEGISMUND: When unjust laws are duly weighed,
            The king, too, may be disobeyed.
            They owed their true prince everything.

2ND SERVANT: His charge was not to reason why
              The king's will isn't sovereign.   1325

SEGISMUND: You must care little for your skin
            To make me constantly reply.

CLARION: Correct, sire! Right the prince is, too!
          It seems like you're the one remiss.

2ND SERVANT: What gives you leave to speak like this?   1330

CLARION: I took the leave myself, man.

SEGISMUND: Who
          On earth are you?

CLARION: A meddling drone
          And chief among that nosy group,
          The best example of a snoop
          Our great wide world has ever known.   1335

SEGISMUND: In this strange realm, I've yet to greet
                  A man who's pleased me more.

CLARION: Kind lord,
                  I aim to please and am adored
                  By every Segismund I meet.

Scene iv

[*Enter* ASTOLF.]

ASTOLF: Oh, ever happy dawns the day   1340
                  When you, the son of Poland, show
                  Your face resplendent and aglow
                  In joyfulness and bright array!
                  You tinge the earth's horizons red;
                  Your crimson mantle hues the skies,   1345
                  For like the morning sun you rise
                  Out some secluded mountain bed.
                  Ascend, however late! Defer
                  No more the crowning of these slopes
                  With laurel leaves the palace hopes   1350
                  Shall never fade.

SEGISMUND: God keep you, sir.

ASTOLF: You might have earned a stern rebuke
                  For having failed to see in time
                  That rank deserves more reverence. I'm
                  The titled Astolf, highborn Duke   1355
                  Of Moscow, cousin to your line.
                  We're equals, each a noble peer.

SEGISMUND: So, when I say "God keep you" here,
                  What does that greeting undermine?
                  Prone as you are to boastful rot   1360

About your name and to complaint,
I'll say without the least restraint
When next we meet, "God keep you not."

2ND SERVANT: Such brusqueness, Highness, still occurs
Throughout his speech and can cause chills,   1365
But then, they raised him in the hills.
The noble Astolf far prefers . . .

SEGISMUND: His smug complacency and strut
Annoyed me greatly. Then to doff
His hat and fail to keep it off . . .   1370

2ND SERVANT: He's royal.

SEGISMUND: But a royal what?

2ND SERVANT: That said, it's fitting there should be
More mutual respect from two
Who aren't mere noblemen.

SEGISMUND: Pray, who
Dispatched you here to torment me?   1375

Scene v

[*Enter* STELLA.]

STELLA: Your Royal Highness, may the throne
Beneath this canopy extend
A welcome that shall never end
To one it proudly claims its own.
And may you reign here free from fears   1380
Of intrigue as our monarch who'll
Augustly and serenely rule
For centuries, not merely years.

SEGISMUND:	Oh tell me, who is that discreet
	And sovereign beauty standing there?	1385
	What human goddess passing fair
	At whose divine, celestial feet
	The skies cast down their crimson light?
	What lovely maid do I admire?

| CLARION: | Your cousin, Lady Stella, sire. | 1390 |

SEGISMUND:	Say "sun" and you'd be no less right.
	How fine of you to wish me well
	With fine-wrought words in this strange
	place.
	Since first I saw that fine-shaped face,
	Your well-wishing has worked its spell	1395
	And as I've come to feel such fine
	Remarks unearned, though gladly heard,
	I'm grateful for the gracious word.
	Sweet Stella, you who rise and shine
	To light the mornings with your rays	1400
	And cheer the radiant orb's bright run,
	What function do you leave the sun
	By rising at the break of days?
	Oh, let me kiss that gorgeous hand,
	A snow-white chalice where the breeze	1405
	Imbibes quintessence at its ease.

| STELLA: | My lord, be courteous in your stand. |

| ASTOLF: | If she succumbs to this, then I |
| | Am lost! |

2ND SERVANT:	I sense good Astolf's pain
	But can I make the prince refrain?	1410
	My lord, I'm sure you fathom why
	This violates court protocol
	With Astolf present . . .

SEGISMUND: Didn't we
                  Agree you'd stop tormenting me?

2ND SERVANT: I said it's not correct.

SEGISMUND: This all   1415
                  Has greatly angered me today!
                  Thwart any outcome I expect
                  And I will deem that incorrect.

2ND SERVANT: But sire, I even heard you say
                  That service and obeyance both   1420
                  Are acts correct beyond compare.

SEGISMUND: I think you also heard me swear
                  I'd throw a nuisance, on my oath,
                  From off this balcony to die.

2ND SERVANT: You can't treat men like me with so   1425
                  Much disregard and scorn.

SEGISMUND: Oh, no?
                  Why don't I just give this a try?

[He grabs the 2ND SERVANT, exits followed by all. SEGISMUND,
ASTOLF, STELLA, and CLARION return.]

ASTOLF: I can't believe what I've just seen!

STELLA: Come quickly and help stop this row!

[She exits.]

SEGISMUND: He plunged into the sea below   1430
                  And God let no one intervene!

ASTOLF: I'd look to moderate these sorts

Of reckless acts and rash pursuits;
Men are no farther from base brutes
Than mountains are from palace courts.   1435

SEGISMUND: Keep talking like some paragon
Of virtue as you lecture me
And, sooner than you think, you'll see
You've naught to place your hat upon.

[*Exit* ASTOLF. *Enter* BASIL.]

Scene vi

BASIL: What's going on here?

SEGISMUND: Not a thing.   1440
I stopped a knave from pestering me
And tossed him off the balcony.

CLARION: Take care, you're talking to the king.

BASIL: Not one day at the palace, yet
Already human life's been lost.   1445

SEGISMUND: He claimed I couldn't, and it cost
Him dear. Looks like I won that bet.

BASIL: It grieves us greatly that our late
Reunion be so villainized.
We'd thought that, having been apprised   1450
Of how the stars have steered your fate,
You might supplant this rage with tact.
And yet, to what do you resort
On first appearing at the court?
A savage, homicidal act.   1455
What kind of fatherly embrace
Could you expect these arms to give

When we could only hope to live
To breathe the air by God's good grace
Far from your murderous grasp? Who could   1460
Behold a naked dagger glow
Before it struck a mortal blow
And fail to shrink in fear? Who would
Bear witness to the blood-red pall
That lingered where a man was killed   1465
And not be moved? The strongest willed
Among us would heed instinct's call.
As we perceive the grievous harms
That issue from your cruel embrace
And contemplate this bloodied place,   1470
We'll keep safe distance from those arms.
So though we'd planned, our love revealed,
To fling these arms about your neck,
We hold these sentiments in check,
Fear-stricken by the might you wield.   1475

SEGISMUND: I've lived outside their fold till now
And don't see what I stand to lose.
A father who would so abuse
Authority to disavow
His own son's birthright merits scorn.   1480
Entombed as if I were deceased,
Raised wild like a savage beast
And treated like some monster born
To forfeit life by your decree,
I hold that clasp for which you yearn   1485
Of no emotional concern—
You robbed me of humanity.

BASIL: By heaven's just omnipotence,
We rue the day we gave you life
To countenance this fiery strife   1490
And tolerate such insolence.

SEGISMUND: Had you not sired me willfully,
             I'd have no basis for complaint,
             But since you did, what need restraint?
             You took my life away from me.   1495
             And while no act is nobler than
             To give, whatever that gift's worth,
             No baser act exists on earth
             Than taking back that gift again.

BASIL: Are these the thanks that lay in store   1500
             For turning a foul prisoner
             Into a prince?

SEGISMUND: I can't infer
             What I've to be so thankful for,
             You tyrant to my will! Malign,
             Decrepit despot! You'll soon breathe   1505
             Your last! What gift do you bequeath
             But that which rightfully is mine?
             Since you're my father and my king,
             The grandeur and nobility
             That Nature's law bestowed on me   1510
             Were mine for the inheriting.
             So in my new exalted state
             And in no way obliged to you,
             I say your day of reckoning's due
             For all the years you'd abrogate   1515
             My honor, life, and liberty.
             You should be thanking me, you know,
             For not collecting what you owe,
             As you, sir, are in debt to me.

BASIL: Impulsive, wild, and barbarous!   1520
             All heaven augured has come true.
             Look down, skies, on his rage and view
             Him utterly contrarious!
             Although our ultimate behest

Disclosed your true identity   1525
And palace graces guarantee
The prince be prized above the rest,
Attend these words for your soul's sake:
Be humble, man, and less extreme,
For all you see might be a dream,   1530
Though you may think you're wide
    awake.

[*He exits.*]

SEGISMUND: What could he mean? I, dreaming, when
All this is patent to my eyes?
I touch, I feel, and can devise
What I am now and was back then.   1535
You may well rue your choices, yet
You're powerless to change them now.
I'm noble, and no matter how
Intently you may feel regret,
No man can ever strip away   1540
The prince and heir apparent's crown.
Though your first sight of me was down
In that dank prison where I lay,
My fast self-knowledge has increased
And now that I've seen through the sham   1545
Of what I was, I know I am
Some mongrel mix of man and beast.

Scene vii

[*Enter* ROSAURA, *dressed as a lady-in-waiting.*]

ROSAURA: Dame Stella wants me near,
Though I'm afraid of meeting Astolf here.
Clotaldo thinks it best   1550
He neither see me nor divine my quest,
As cleansing honor warrants sacrifice.

I trust his sage advice,
Indebted as I am to he who came
And rescued both my life and honored name.   1555

CLARION: [*To* SEGISMUND.] So, which among the host
Of things you've seen today has pleased you
    most?

SEGISMUND: I wasn't much surprised
By anything. All was as I'd surmised.
But since you have inquired,   1560
The thing on earth that's most to be admired
Is woman's beauty. Mind
Me now: I'd read, while odiously confined,
That out of all the creatures in His plan,
God spent most time on that small
    cosmos, man.   1565
But this cannot be true,
For woman is a slice of heaven, too,
And lovelier by far,
As distant from male clay as earth from star,
Like her I now behold.   1570

ROSAURA: The prince! I must withdraw and be less bold.

SEGISMUND: I beg you, woman, stay.
Don't make the sun set at the break of day
By leaving on the run.
You'll blend the dawn and twilight into one,   1575
Cold dark with sunbeams bright,
And cut too short the shining of the light.
Wait! What's this I perceive?

ROSAURA: I can't trust my own eyes, yet must believe.

SEGISMUND: I've seen this loveliness   1580
Before.

ROSAURA: And I this grandeur, though with less
                        Solemnity back when
                        It lay in chains.

SEGISMUND: I've found my life again!
                        Speak, woman—yes, I use
                        The most endearing term a man can choose— 1585
                        Who are you? Have we met?
                        No matter; you owe me allegiance, yet
                        Some strange bond links us more.
                        I'm certain that I've seen your face before.
                        Who are you, woman fair?   1590

ROSAURA: [*Aside.*] I must pretend. [*To* SEGISMUND.]
                            A lady wrought with care
                        Who serves in Stella's train.

SEGISMUND: No, say you are the sun, in whose domain
                        Of fire the stellar bides,
                        For Stella basks in rays your light provides.   1595
                        In all the fragrant realm
                        Of flowers, there's but one goddess at the
                            helm,
                        The rose, whom others call
                        Their empress, being loveliest of all.
                        I've seen the finest stones   1600
                        Extracted from the earth's profoundest zones
                        Revere the diamond's shine,
                        Their emperor as brightest in the mine.
                        At lush courts in the sky
                        Where stars from teetering republics vie,   1605
                        I've seen fair Venus reign
                        As queen of all that vast and starred
                            demesne.
                        In those ethereal climes,
                        I've seen the sun convene the orbs oftimes
                        At court, where he holds sway,   1610

Presiding as the oracle of day.
How could a case arise,
Then, where the planets, stones, and flowers
   prize
Great beauty, yet yours serves
A lady far less fair? Your charm deserves   1615
More praise than hers bestows,
Oh, bright sun, Venus, diamond, star, and
   rose!

Scene viii

[*Enter* CLOTALDO.]

CLOTALDO: Restraining Segismund devolves on me,
              As he was once my ward. What's this I see?

ROSAURA: I'm flattered by your praise,   1620
              Though silence plies a lofty turn of phrase,
              For when a person's judgment seems most
                 blurred,
              The best response is not to say a word.

SEGISMUND: You musn't go yet. Wait!
              You wouldn't want to leave in such a state,   1625
              Misjudging my desire?

ROSAURA: I beg permission, Highness, to retire.

SEGISMUND: Your veiled demands aggrieve;
              You don't so much request as take your
                 leave.

ROSAURA: What choice have I when you won't
                 let me pass?
                                         1630

SEGISMUND: I'm civil now, but might become more crass

Soon, for resistance strains
My patience like a poison in my veins!

ROSAURA: Not even poison laced
With fury so intensive it effaced   1635
This patience you declare
Could ever stain my honor, nor would dare.

SEGISMUND: You're trying hard, I see,
To make yourself appear less fair to me.
You'll always find me game   1640
To take on the impossible. The claim
Some knave made that I couldn't cause his
  death
Was breathed with his last breath,
So if I dared to probe all I could do,
I'd throw your honor out the window,
  too!   1645

CLOTALDO: His rage will not relent.
What should I do, dear heavens, with him bent
Upon this lustful crime,
Imperiling my name a second time?

ROSAURA: The fateful prophecy   1650
That warned this kingdom of your tyranny
Foresaw the crimes you'd bear,
The scandal, murder, treason, and despair.
Still, who could stoop to blame
A human being who's just a man in name,   1655
Cruel, reckless, inhumane,
A barbarous tyrant no one can restrain,
Reared like some savage beast?

SEGISMUND: I'd thought my wooing at the very least
Would spare me this display   1660
And hoped to win your favor in this way.

But since my suit occasions such alarm,
See what you think of me without the
      charm!
Leave us, the lot of you, and bolt the door.
See no one enters here.

[*Exit* CLARION.]

ROSAURA: I die for sure!   1665
                    Wait . . .

SEGISMUND: Fleeing my embrace
                    Will hardly put this tyrant in his place.

CLOTALDO: Again he kindles strife!
                    I hope this meddling won't cost me my life.
                    Desist, sire! Let her be.   1670

SEGISMUND: This is the second time you've angered me,
                    You doddering old dunce.
                    Have you no fear you'll pay for these
                          affronts?
                    How did you slip in here?

CLOTALDO: I entered, summoned by these tones of fear,   1675
                    To urge you to restrain
                    Such impulse if you ever wish to reign.
                    You're not king yet, so temper this extreme
                    Behavior. All you see may be a dream.

SEGISMUND: You know I grow irate   1680
                    When you use fantasy to set me straight.
                    Would it be dream to slay
                    You or quite real?

[As SEGISMUND *draws his sword,* CLOTALDO *grabs his arm
and kneels before him.*]

CLOTALDO: I know no other way
                  To save my life, my lord!

SEGISMUND: How dare you place your hands
                  upon my sword?   1685

CLOTALDO: I won't release this blade
                  Until a body comes to give me aid
                  And calm your rage.

ROSAURA: My God!

SEGISMUND: Let go, I said,
                  You senile fool, or you're as good as dead!
                  If you continue so, [*They struggle.*]   1690
                  I'll crush you in my arms, detested foe!

ROSAURA: Who'll help us? Anyone!
                  Clotaldo's being killed!

[*She exits.* ASTOLF *enters,* CLOTALDO *falls at his feet, and* AS-
TOLF *steps between* CLOTALDO *and* SEGISMUND.]

Scene ix

ASTOLF: What have you done
                  To him, good-hearted lord?
                  Cold blood should never blight so
                  brave a sword   1695
                  With stains of infamy.
                  Resheathe your blade and let the old man be.

SEGISMUND: I will when his depraved
                  Blood tinges it bright red.

ASTOLF: His life is saved—
                  He's sued for sanctuary at my feet   1700

And not to spear him, sire, would scarce be
    meet.

SEGISMUND: Allow me, then, to spare your life as well
So I might have revenge for what befell
Me earlier at your hands.

ASTOLF: No self-defense
Could cause judicious majesty offense.   1705

Scene x

[ASTOLF *and* SEGISMUND *draw their swords. Enter King*
BASIL *and* STELLA.]

CLOTALDO: Don't injure him!

BASIL: What, drawn before
    the king?

STELLA: It's Astolf, furious and battling!

BASIL: Just what is happening here?

ASTOLF: Sire, not a thing now that Your Grace
    is near.

[ASTOLF *and* SEGISMUND *sheathe their swords.*]

SEGISMUND: A great deal, sire, be you near or not.   1710
I'd just begun to murder this old sot.

BASIL: Why, was no reverence shown
For these gray hairs?

CLOTALDO: My liege, they're
                                  mine alone
              And little matter.

SEGISMUND: Nothing you could say
              Would force me to respect that hoary gray   1715
              And all its vile deceit.
              I'll see it someday, too, beneath my feet,
              Which may at last avenge
              My stolen life and bring me sweet revenge.

    [He exits.]

BASIL: Before you see these things,   1720
              You'll sleep again, and all the happenings
              You'd once believed were real
              Will only prove to be what dreams reveal.

    [Exit BASIL and CLOTALDO.]

Scene xi

ASTOLF: The stars above so rarely lie
              When they predict catastrophes.   1725
              They forecast ills with acumen
              But blessings hesitatingly.
              How famous an astrologer
              Would that man be who only spied
              Disasters, for, without a doubt,   1730
              These always manage to transpire!
              My life and Segismund's attest
              To this contrivance of the stars,
              Which presaged for the two of us
              Divergent fortunes from the start.   1735
              For him, they foresaw misery,
              Misfortune, insolence, and death.
              As all these have been evident,

The stars have since been proved correct.
For me, though, lady, once I'd gazed   1740
Upon your eyes' unrivaled beams—
Beside which sunshine looks like shade
And light from heaven epicene—
They seemed to foretell gladdened times
Of triumph, comfort, and acclaim,   1745
Which proved to be both true and false
Because stars only forecast fates
With accuracy when they turn
The joy they bode to wretchedness.

STELLA: I've no doubt that these gallant words   1750
               Are spoken with the best intent
               But you must mean them for the maid
               Whose painted likeness hung about
               Your neck, good Astolf, first you
                 came
               To visit me and seek the crown.   1755
               As this is so, these sentiments
               Belong to her, and her alone.
               Go seek sweet recompense from her
               Because, as promissory notes,
               The courtly grace and oaths of faith   1760
               You use as currency to serve
               For other maids and other kings
               Are worthless in love's constant world.

Scene xii

[*Enter* ROSAURA, *not seen by* STELLA *and* ASTOLF.]

ROSAURA: [*Aside.*] Thank heavens my calamitous
               Adversity has reached its end!   1765
               Whoever's seen what I've seen should
               Have nothing more to fear again!

ASTOLF: I'll take her portrait from my chest
               And lovingly hang in its place
               The image of your loveliness.   1770
               For where fair Stella shines, no shade
               Can fall, no lowly star besmirch
               The sun's bright realm! I'll fetch it now.
               Oh, fair Rosaura, pardon this
               Transgression, but you aren't around.   1775
               When men and women are apart,
               Their troth is worth no more than this.

    [*He exits.*]

ROSAURA: Because I feared I might be seen,
               I hid and couldn't hear a thing.

STELLA: Astrea!

ROSAURA: Yes, fair lady mine.   1780

STELLA: How very much my heart's consoled
               To find you here of all my train,
               For I could think to bare my soul
               To no one else.

ROSAURA: You honor one
               Whose only wish has been to please.   1785

STELLA: Astrea, I can scarcely claim
               I know you, yet you hold the key
               To opening my inmost heart.
               Because of all you clearly are,
               I'll risk confiding to you what   1790
               I've long been keeping in the dark
               From my own self.

ROSAURA: I'm here to serve.

STELLA: Then, let me keep the story brief.
My cousin Astolf—cousin, sure!
Why say he's so much more to me   1795
When some things are as good as said
In thought, where wishes are fulfilled?—
Yes, Astolf and I are to wed
If it should be the heavens' will
To undo countless miseries   1800
By granting us this happiness.
A lady's portrait that he wore
About his neck when we first met
So saddened me, I gently pressed
To know the maid's identity.   1805
A gallant man, he loves me well
And has withdrawn now to retrieve
The likeness. Modesty forbids
My being here on his return,
So wait for him and, when he comes,   1810
Request he leave the miniature
With you. For now, I'll say no more.
Your beauty and discretion show
That you'll soon know what love is, too.

[*She exits.*]

Scene xiii

ROSAURA: I wish to God I'd never known!   1815
Just heavens, help me now! Is there
A woman anywhere alive
Whose artfulness could find a means
To rescue her from such a bind?
Have those inclement skies above   1820
Oppressed a lady so before,
Assailing her with ceaseless grief
Until she's wretched and forlorn?
My delicate predicament

Makes it impossible for me   1825
To be consoled by arguments
Or counseled on my miseries,
As ever since that first mischance
Befell me, not one incident's
Occurred that hasn't brought me grief.   1830
This sad succession of events,
All heirs apparent of themselves,
Arise like phoenixes from ash
As each, newborn, begets the next.
They come to life mid smoldering death,   1835
The cinders of this renaissance
Their sepulcher and birthing bed.
"Our cares are cowards, and poltroons,"
A certain sage was wont to say,
"Stalk humans cravenly in packs."   1840
But I declare misfortunes brave
For always forging nobly on
And never beating weak retreats.
Whoever has experienced
The strain of care may face life free   1845
Of worries or the nagging fear
That cares will ever leave his side.
I know this far too well from all
The woes inflicted on my life
And can't recall a time when cares   1850
Were absent. They'll refuse to rest
Till I succumb, a casualty
Of fate, into the arms of death.
What choice would any woman have
If she were in my place?   1855
Disclosing my identity
Might cause Clotaldo great offense,
For he's vouchsafed my refuge, life,
And honor under great duress.
By keeping silence, he believes,   1860
I'll see my honored name restored,

But if I don't say who I am
When Astolf spies me here at court,
How will I feign not knowing him?
For even if my voice and eyes   1865
Unite to fake their ignorance,
My soul would give them all the lie.
So what am I to do? Why plan
Contrivances when it's so plain
To see that, notwithstanding all   1870
The thought I'd given to prepare
For my encountering him again,
This heartache will respond the way
It pleases? Who among us boasts
Dominion over all his pain?   1875
So with a soul too timorous
To dare determine what my course
Should be, oh, may my heartache end
Today, may all the pains I've borne
Desist, and may I leave behind   1880
Both semblances that once deceived
And lingering doubt. But until then,
Sweet heavens, stand guard over me!

Scene xiv

[*Enter* ASTOLF *with the portrait.*]

ASTOLF: Fair lady, here's the portrait you . . .
                 My God, what's this?

ROSAURA: My lord appears   1885
                 Amazed. What causes his surprise?

ASTOLF: Beholding you, Rosaura, here.

ROSAURA: Rosaura? Why, Your Lordship is
                 Confused and certainly mistakes

Me for another maid. I'm called   1890
Astrea, and my humble state
Could scarcely captivate a duke
Or bring such rapture to my life.

ASTOLF: Rosaura, let this pretense end.
               You know the soul can never lie;   1895
               Though I may see Astrea here,
               I'll love her like Rosaura yet.

ROSAURA: I comprehend you not, my lord,
               Hence my replies are hesitant.
               I'll only say that I was bid   1900
               By Stella, Venus's star here,
               To tarry in this place until
               Such time as you, my lord, appeared
               To ask from you on her behalf
               The portrait causing her such hurt—   1905
               An understandable demand—
               Which I would then remit to her.
               My lady's pleasure wills it so;
               However small the pleas she makes,
               Though they be to my detriment,   1910
               Are Stella's still, and I obey.

ASTOLF: Say what you will, Rosaura, though
               You're terrible at subterfuge.
               Go tell that music in your eyes
               To play in concert with the tune   1915
               Your voice sings so their melody
               Might temper this discordant clash
               And harmonize their instrument,
               Adjusting measures in the dance
               Of all the falsehoods that you speak   1920
               And that one verity you feel.

ROSAURA: Let me repeat, I wait but for
                 The portrait.

ASTOLF: Very well. I see
               You won't forsake this pretense, so
               I'll answer, then, with one my own.   1925
               Astrea, given my esteem
               For Stella, let the lady know
               That my obliging her request
               To fetch this pendant seems a poor
               Example of gentility.   1930
               Hence, as she is so well-adored,
               I send her the original,
               Which you may bear her in the flesh,
               Revealing the extent to which
               You and the likeness are enmeshed.   1935

ROSAURA: A man who sets out bold and brave
               To bring back something on his word
               And then returns not with this prize
               But with some thing of greater worth
               Conceded him, still thinks himself   1940
               A slighted fool whose mission failed.
               I'd hoped to take my portrait back
               Though the original won't pale
               In force beside it. Still, I can't
               Return so slighted. Come, my lord,   1945
               You'll hand the portrait over now—
               Without it I must shun the court.

ASTOLF: And if I don't relinquish this,
               What will you then?

ROSAURA: All-out assault—
               Let go of it!

ASTOLF: You strike in vain.   1950

ROSAURA: The portrait mustn't ever fall
                Into another woman's hands.

ASTOLF: You're spirited!

ROSAURA: False-hearted cheat!

ASTOLF: That's quite enough, Rosaura mine.

ROSAURA: I yours, you scoundrel? You're deceived!   1955

Scene xv

[*Enter* STELLA.]

STELLA: Astrea! Astolf! What's all this?

ASTOLF: Now Lady Stella's come.

ROSAURA: [*Aside.*] Oh, Love,
                Grant me the prowess to retrieve
                My portrait! Lady, if you want
                To know why we are quarreling,   1960
                I'll tell you.

ASTOLF: What's the point of this?

ROSAURA: You bade me, lady, tarry here
                For Astolf so he might remit
                To me the portrait you desired.
                Well, once I found myself alone—   1965
                The mind can traipse so easily
                Through scores of subjects, as you know—
                This talk of portraits drifted back

To jog my memory, as it would,
Till I recalled my sleeve bore one   1970
Of me, and thought I'd take a look—
For when no one's around, we must
Amuse ourselves with what is near—
But then I dropped the thing just as
Duke Astolf presently appeared   1975
To bring the other portrait by.
He picked mine up, but so resists
Complying with the charge he's borne
That now he says he'll harbor it
Along with yours. Despite my pleas,   1980
He won't consent to hand mine back.
Your Ladyship came just in time
To see me in the frenzied act
Of repossessing it by force.
The portrait dangling in his grasp   1985
Is mine, which you could verify,
My lady, with a simple glance.

STELLA: You may return her miniature.

[*She takes it from him.*]

ASTOLF: My lady . . .

STELLA: Yes, I must allow   1990
It almost does you justice, maid.

ROSAURA: You see it's mine, then?

STELLA: I've no doubt.

ROSAURA: Now ask him for the other one.

STELLA: Please take your portrait and retire.

ROSAURA: [*Aside.*] Why should I care what
                    happens next
                As long as I've reclaimed what's mine?   1995

[*She exits.*]

Scene xvi

STELLA: I'd like the portrait that I asked
                You for. I'll never lay my eyes
                On you or speak to you again.
                Still, knowing it remains your prized
                Possession pains me to no end,   2000
                Not least because I fondly did
                Petition it.

ASTOLF: [*Aside.*] What's there to say
                In such confused predicaments?
                    [*To* STELLA.]
                Fair Stella, I'm your servant still
                In every possible regard.   2005
                It's just not in my power now
                To grant your wish because . . .

STELLA: You are
                A faithless lover and vile man.
                Forget I asked for it at all;
                Why should I want her portrait when   2010
                The very sight of it recalls
                My having had to plead for it?

[*She exits.*]

ASTOLF: Don't go! Please listen! Give me time,
                Rosaura! Dear Lord, grant me strength!
                Just how, from where, for what and why   2015

Did you turn up in Poland now
To seek your ruin as well as mine?

[*He exits.*]

Scene xvii

[SEGISMUND *appears as he did at play's start, wearing animal pelts and in chains, asleep on the ground. Enter* CLOTALDO, CLARION, *and two servants.*]

CLOTALDO: Just leave him drowsing on the ground.
Today his overweening pride
Will end where it began.

1ST SERVANT: I've tried   2020
To chain him as he'd once been bound.

CLARION: Why rush to wake and be decrowned
When sleeping, Segismund, will save
Yourself the sight of fortune's knave?
The glory you've enjoyed is fled   2025
And you'll endure, alive but dead,
A specter from beyond the grave.

CLOTALDO: An orator with this much flair
Will also need a cloistered space,
Some quiet, isolated place   2030
Where he might discourse free of care.
Go seize that speechifier there
And lock him in his tower retreat.

CLARION: Why me?

CLOTALDO: Because it's understood
That clarions left unmuffled could   2035

                Sound off and noisily repeat
                Our palace secrets in the street.

CLARION: Do I, perchance, plot endlessly
                To murder my own father? No!
                Was I the one who dared to throw   2040
                That sorry Icarus in the sea?
                Am I reborn or still just me?
                Is this a bad dream? Why this plan
                To jail me?

CLOTALDO: Your name's Clarion, man.

CLARION: Then during my imprisonment   2045
                I'll be a viler instrument,
                The cornet, and stay mute a span.

[*The servants take* CLARION *away.*]

Scene xviii

[*Enter King* BASIL, *disguised.*]

BASIL: Clotaldo.

CLOTALDO: Sire! Does this disguise
                Befit your Royal Majesty?

BASIL: The foolish curiosity   2050
                To view the prince with our own eyes
                And see the state in which he lies
                Has led us to his cell today.

CLOTALDO: Just look at him there, brought to bay
                In chains, dejected and forlorn.   2055

BASIL: The star beneath which you were born
                 Determined it would be this way.
                 Go wake him. So much for our schemes.
                 The drink you brewed has run its course
                 And all its herbs have lost their force.   2060

CLOTALDO: His sleep is restless, yet he seems
                 To speak.

BASIL: What manner of strange dreams
                 Could visit Segismund alone?

SEGISMUND: [*In his world of dream.*] A pious
                      prince is one who's known
                 For purging tyrants from his lands.   2065
                 Clotaldo dies by these two hands
                 While Basil, prostrate, yields his throne.

CLOTALDO: My dying makes the plot complete.

BASIL: He joins effrontery with threat.

CLOTALDO: He'll see me foully murdered yet.   2070

BASIL: And vanquish us beneath his feet.

SEGISMUND: [*Still dreaming.*] Parade your valor in
                      the street,
                 The world's great theater, onstage where
                 Its size will loom beyond compare.
                 Avenging my base sire's neglect   2075
                 Will only have the right effect
                 If Segismund's triumphant there.
                      [*He awakens.*]
                 What's this about? Where can I be?

BASIL: He's not to learn that we're here, too.
                    Now do what you've been charged to do   2080
                    As we retire where we can see.

[*He withdraws from view.*]

SEGISMUND: What's happened? Is this really me
                    In chains again amid this blight,
                    A horrid and pathetic sight?
                    And is that you, my living tomb,   2085
                    Old tower? God help me meet this doom!
                    But what strange things I dreamt tonight!

CLOTALDO: I'm duty bound to keep this mime
                    Alive, whatever it may take.
                    Is it not time for you to wake?   2090

SEGISMUND: Yes, it's well past my waking time.

CLOTALDO: Do you intend to spend the prime
                    Of day asleep? Can it be right
                    That, ever since we tracked the flight
                    Of that grand eagle heaven bound,   2095
                    You've lain here drowsing on the ground
                    And never once awakened?

SEGISMUND: Quite,
                    And haven't yet, as I'd conceived.
                    As far as I can ascertain,
                    I sleepwalk still through dream's domain   2100
                    And would not feel at all deceived
                    If everything that I'd believed
                    Took place would dissipate anew
                    Or if what I saw now weren't true.
                    For one in chains, it's no great leap   2105
                    To understand, though fast asleep,
                    That one can dream while waking, too.

CLOTALDO: What did you dream while so confined?

SEGISMUND: Supposing that it was a dream,
                 Clotaldo! Here is what I deem   2110
                 Occurred, and not just in my mind:
                 I wakened yesterday to find
                 Myself—this taunts me!—lounging in
                 A bed so bright it might have been
                 The flowery cot by which the Spring   2115
                 Adorns the earth with coloring
                 From all the hues contained therein.
                 A thousand nobles bowed before
                 My vaunted feet and, once they'd hailed
                 Me as their prince, I was regaled   2120
                 With banquets, jewels, robes, and more.
                 You purged what calm my senses bore
                 By naming me, to my delight,
                 King Basil's heir by natural right
                 And though my fortune's fallen since,   2125
                 I briefly reigned as Poland's prince.

CLOTALDO: What great reward had I in sight?

SEGISMUND: Accusing you of treachery,
                 My heart made bold with power and vice,
                 I tried disposing of you twice.   2130

CLOTALDO: But why were you so cruel to me?

SEGISMUND: I'd thought to rule with tyranny
                 And match the evil I'd been done.
                 I loved none but one woman—one—
                 The only real thing to transcend,   2135
                 As I believe, my dreaming's end,
                 An endless need that's just begun.

[BASIL *exits*.]

CLOTALDO: [*Aside.*] The king was moved by
           what he heard
      And fled affected from the tower.
      Our talk in your last waking hour   2140
      About that eagle must have spurred
      These dreams of empire afterward.
      Still, Segismund, you really ought
      To honor one who reared and taught
      You, even in the realm of dream.   2145
      For doing good is man's supreme
      Imperative and not for naught.

[*He exits.*]

Scene xix

SEGISMUND: How very true! Then let's suppress
      The fury of our savage state,
      The vile ambition and the hate,   2150
      So when we dream we won't transgress.
      For dream we will, though we possess
      No sense of where it is we thrive
      And dreaming just means being alive.
      The insight life's experience gives   2155
      Is that, until man wakes, he lives
      A life that only dreams contrive.
      The king dreams he is king and reigns
      Deluded in his full command,
      Imposing order in his land.   2160
      The borrowed plaudits he obtains
      Blow scattered through the wind's domains
      As death—man's life is so unjust!—
      Transmutes them into ash and dust.
      Oh, who on earth could wish to wield   2165
      Such might when waking means to yield
      It all to death's dream, as we must?
      The rich man dreams his riches great,

Which makes his wealth more burdensome.
The poor man dreams that he'll succumb   2170
To misery in his beggared state.
He also dreams who prospers late.
The striver and aspirer do,
The mocker and offender, too.
In fact, all mortal souls on earth   2175
Dream their conditions from their birth,
Though no one knows this to be true.
I'm dreaming now that darker days
Await me, chained, in this dark cell
As I'd dreamt I'd been treated well   2180
Of late in some strange coddled phase.
What's life? A frenzied, blurry haze.
What's life? Not anything it seems.
A shadow. Fiction filling reams.
All we possess on earth means nil,   2185
For life's a dream, think what you will,
And even all our dreams are dreams.

ACT III

Scene i

[*Enter* CLARION.]

CLARION: I lodge in this enchanted tower
A captive, for I know the truth,
But if my knowledge means sure death,   2190
What will my ignorance lead to?
That such a hungry, hungry man
Should perish like a living corpse!
I'm feeling sorry for myself,
So go ahead, say, "That's for sure,"   2195
For surely, that's not hard to see.
This silence, too, is pretty rough,
But when your name is Clarion, well,
There's just no way to hold your tongue.
My sole companions in this place—   2200
And this would be a wild guess—
Are mice and spiders lurking here.
Who needs a goldfinch for a pet?
My teeming brain is still awhirl
With everything I dreamt last night: 2205
The sound of trumpet blares and shawms
Came mingled with deceptive sights
Like one of flagellants that marched
In some procession of the cross,
First rising, then descending, then   2210

Succumbing once they saw the lost
Blood flowing down their fellows' backs.
These bouts with hunger here of late
May cause the swoons in me as well,
For, while I'm left to starve by day,   2215
An empty Plato offers no
Consolement of philosophy,
While each night I appear before
A Diet of Worms, which isn't meet.
So if this new Church calendar   2220
Considers silence "blessed" now,
Let Secret be my patron saint—
I'll fast for him and break no vows.
I haven't breathed a word yet, so
My punishment seems well deserved: 2225
What greater sacrilege is there
Than quiet from one hired to serve?

Scene ii

[*The sound of drums and soldiers' voices offstage.*]

1ST SOLDIER: They're holding him inside this tower.
                Here, batter down these bolted doors
                And storm the cell!

CLARION: Good heavens, have   2230
                They come for me? I'm pretty sure,
                Since they seem pretty sure I'm here.
                Whatever could they want?

1ST SOLDIER: Charge in!

2ND SOLDIER: He's here!

CLARION: Oh, no he's not!

SOLDIERS: [*To* CLARION.] My lord!

CLARION: They must be drunkards on a binge!   2235

2ND SOLDIER: All hail, our prince and rightful liege!
                 To you alone do we submit
                 Our forces, natural-born heir,
                 And not to any foreign prince.
                 To prove our troth, we kiss your feet.   2240

SOLDIERS: Long live the prince, whom we love well!

CLARION: Good God, can this be happening?
                 Is it the custom in this realm
                 To seize a body every day
                 And make a prince of him before   2245
                 He's thrown back in the tower? Must be,
                 Since each day there's a different lord.
                 Looks like I'll have to play the part.

SOLDIERS: Give us your feet!

CLARION: I can't because
                 I need to use them for myself   2250
                 And it would be a tragic flaw
                 To govern as a soleless prince.

2ND SOLDIER: We've seen your father and declared
                 Our will to him: it's you alone
                 We recognize as Poland's heir,   2255
                 And not the Muscovite.

CLARION: You told
                 My father? Have you no respect,
                 You lousy bunch of so-and-so's?

1ST SOLDIER: One can't keep loyal hearts in check.

| CLARION: | Well, loyalty I can excuse. | 2260 |

| 2ND SOLDIER: | Restore the kingdom to your line.
Long live Prince Segismund! |

| SOLDIERS: | Long life! |

| CLARION: | Ah, they said "Segismund." All right,
So Segismund's the word they use
To mean a prince is counterfeit. | 2265 |

[*Enter* SEGISMUND.]

Scene iii

| SEGISMUND: | Is someone calling out my name? |

| CLARION: | Am I a has-been as a prince? |

| 2ND SOLDIER: | Who here is Segismund? |

| SEGISMUND: | I am. |

| 2ND SOLDIER: | You reckless fool! Impersonate
The heir apparent to the throne? | 2270 |

| CLARION: | Now that's a game I'd never play.
Besides, it was the lot of you
That segismundized me. Ergo,
The only foolish recklessness
Put on display here was your own. | 2275 |

| 1ST SOLDIER: | Great prince, brave Segismund! Although
The standards that we bear are yours,
It's solemn faith alone compels
Our number to proclaim you lord. |

Your father Basil, our great king,   2280
Has lived in terror of the skies
Fulfilling their dread prophecy
That presaged you would see him lie
Subdued beneath your feet. For this,
He'd planned to yield your titled claim   2285
And highborn right to Astolf, Duke
Of Moscow, and eclipse your reign.
King Basil had convened the court
When Poland learned an heir survived
And wished him to succeed the king,   2290
Reluctant that a foreign line
Should govern them on native soil.
So, holding the inclemency
Of starry fate in noble scorn,
They sought your cell to see you freed   2295
From these cruel chains. All live in hope
The rightful heir will leave these grounds
And, buttressed by their arms, reclaim
For them the scepter and the crown
Out that usurping tyrant's grip!   2300
Come forth! Amid this barrenness
An army, sizable and strong,
Of bandits and staunch citizens
Acclaims you. Longed-for liberty
Awaits you, hear its beckoning call!   2305

VOICES: [*Offstage.*] Long live Prince Segismund!
                       All hail!

SEGISMUND: What's this? Must I be held enthralled
                       Again, cruel skies, to fleeting dreams
                       Of grandeur Time will surely mock?
                       Must I again be forced to glimpse   2310
                       Amid the shadows and the fog
                       The majesty and faded pomp
                       That waft inconstant on the wind?

Must I again be left to face
Life's disillusion or the risks   2315
To which man's limits are exposed
From birth and never truly end?
This cannot be. It cannot be.
Behold me here, a slave again
To fortune's whims. As I have learned   2320
That life is really just a dream,
I say to you, false shadows, Go!
My deadened senses know your schemes,
To feign a body and a voice
When voice and body both are shams.   2325
I've no desire for majesty
That's phony or for pompous flam,
Illusions of sheer fantasy
That can't withstand the slightest breeze
And dissipate entirely like   2330
The blossoms on an almond tree
That bloom too early in the spring
Without a hint to anyone.
The beauty, light, and ornament
Reflecting from their rosy buds   2335
Fade all too soon; these wilt and fall
When but the gentlest gusts blow by.
I know you all too well, I do,
To fancy you'd act otherwise
Toward other souls who likewise sleep.   2340
So let this vain pretending cease;
I'm disabused of all I thought
And know now life is but a dream.

2ND SOLDIER: We have not come here to deceive.
Just cast your eyes upon the lair   2345
Of haughty hills that ring this tower
And see the host of men prepared
To follow and obey you.

SEGISMUND: Once
                    I saw the same approving crowd
                    Appear before me as distinct   2350
                    And clear as I perceive things now,
                    But I was dreaming.

2ND SOLDIER: Great events
                    Are oft preceded, good my lord,
                    By portents, which is what occurred
                    When you did dream these things before.   2355

SEGISMUND: A portent. Yes, you must be right.
                    If all is truly as you've deemed
                    And man's life, sadly, is so short,
                    Then let us dream, my soul, let's dream
                    Again! But this time we will face   2360
                    Full recognition of the fact
                    That we may waken from this sleep
                    At any hour and be brought back.
                    Still, knowing such things in advance
                    Should temper disappointment's stings;   2365
                    To put the cure before the harm
                    Does much to mock the injuring.
                    In short, as all have been forewarned
                    That, even when man's sway seems sure,
                    Our power is borrowed on this earth   2370
                    And harks back always to its source,
                    What can we lose by venturing?
                    I thank you, vassals, for this show
                    Of loyalty. With all my skill
                    And bravery I'll smash this yoke   2375
                    Of foreign slavery you fear!
                    Come, sound the call to arms. This
                        sword
                    Will vouch my courage is no lie.
                    It's my intent to levy war

Against my father, proving thus   2380
That heaven prophesied the truth.
I'll see him prone beneath my feet—
Unless I wake before I do,
In which case it might just be best
To say no more about these plans.   2385

ALL: All hail to you, Prince Segismund!

Scene iv

[*Enter* CLOTALDO.]

CLOTALDO: Good heavens, what's this uproar, man?

SEGISMUND: Clotaldo.

CLOTALDO: Sire. [*Aside.*] He's sure to vent
                  His rage upon me now.

CLARION: I bet
                  He throws the codger off this cliff.   2390

[*He exits.*]

CLOTALDO: I bow to you, though I expect
                  To die here at your feet.

SEGISMUND: Pray stand,
                  Good father. Rise up from the ground,
                  My polestar and sole guiding light!
                  You coaxed my better nature out   2395
                  And well I know the debt you're owed
                  For rearing me so faithfully.
                  Let me embrace you.

CLOTALDO: How is that?

SEGISMUND: I'm dreaming now, but in my dream
                I'm striving to do good. No chance   2400
                To do kind deeds should be ignored.

CLOTALDO: My lord, since you profess these acts
                Of grace as your new creed, I'm sure
                You'll take no great offense with me
                For likewise cleaving to these views.   2405
                Wage war against your father? Then
                I simply cannot counsel you
                And aid the downfall of my king.
                So slay me, humbled still upon
                This ground you tread.

SEGISMUND: Oh, traitor! Vile,   2410
                Ungrateful wretch! Almighty God!
                Some self-command might serve me well
                Until it's certain that I wake.
                I envy your stouthearted show,
                Clotaldo. Thank you for this faith.   2415
                Go, then, and serve the king you love;
                We'll meet upon the battle lines.
                All others, sound the call to arms!

CLOTALDO: I kiss your feet a thousand times.

SEGISMUND: Come, Fortune! Off we go to reign,   2420
                So dare not wake me if I sleep
                Nor let me sleep should this be true,
                For whether I now sleep or dream
                It's vital still that man do good
                In dream or sleep for good's own sake,   2425
                At least to win himself some friends
                For when he ultimately wakes.

[*All exit as the call to arms sounds.*]

Scene v

[*Enter King* BASIL *and* ASTOLF.]

BASIL: Good Astolf, who can stop a bolting horse
                And still its rage into serenity?
                Or check a surging river's headlong course   2430
                Before its waters flow into the sea?
                Or halt a falling boulder gathering force
                While hurtling down a mountain fast and free?
                Yet, none of these is harder to arrest
                Than masses who feel angered and
                    oppressed.   2435
                Divulge by edict any news from court
                And all at once you'll hear the echoes sound
                Throughout the hills, as anguished cries
                    exhort
                "Hail Astolf" while "Hail Segismunds"
                    resound.
                Our throne room has been turned into
                    a sort   2440
                Of second stage where horrid plays abound,
                A baneful theater where fate flaunts her will
                And only tragedy is on the bill.

ASTOLF: Then, sire, I will assuredly delay this cause
                For celebration proffered by your hand   2445
                And shun both flattery and loud applause,
                For Poland, where I'd looked to rule as
                    planned,
                Resists my reign today and flouts your laws
                So I might prove my worth to lead the land.
                Bring me a steed whose spirit knows no like;   2450
                You've heard me thunder, now watch
                    lightning strike!

[*He exits.*]

BASIL: No one escapes the inescapable
                  Or any danger omens have in store.
                  Resisting fortune is impossible;
                  Ignoring forecasts just makes them
                      more sure.   2455
                  In our case, this harsh law looms terrible
                  As fleeing danger brings one to its door.
                  Base ruin now appears our secret's cost,
                  For we're alone to blame now Poland's lost.

Scene vi

[*Enter* STELLA.]

STELLA: If your wise presence, sire, can't stop
                      the spread   2460
                  Of opposition forces gaining ground
                  While ever more combative factions head
                  Throughout our streets and plazas, palace
                      bound,
                  You'll see the realm awash in waves of red,
                  Your subjects bathing in the blood
                      now found   2465
                  But in their crimson veins. What tragic
                      gloom
                  Surrounds our kingdom's decadence and
                      doom!
                  To sense the downfall of your rule so near
                  Amid the savage violence of this plot
                  Astounds the eye and terrifies the ear.   2470
                  The wind grows still, the sun turns to a blot;
                  Each rock will be a headstone to revere,
                  Each flower the marker on a fresh grave's
                      spot,
                  Each edifice a lofty house of death,
                  Each soldier but a skeleton with breath.   2475

Scene vii

[*Enter* CLOTALDO.]

CLOTALDO: I've made it here alive, for God is kind.

BASIL: Clotaldo, have you news about our son?

CLOTALDO: The masses, sire, a monster rash and blind,
              Besieged the tower and, seeing it overrun,
              Freed Segismund. No sooner did he find   2480
              A second time this second honor won
              Than out he burst emboldened and uncouth,
              Resolved to prove the heavens spoke the
                   truth.

BASIL: Bring us a steed, for as your king we must
              Defeat this ingrate out of royal pride.   2485
              But this time in our crown's defense we'll
                   trust
              Cold steel where once our hapless science
                   vied.

     [*He exits.*]

STELLA: Bright sun, I'll be Bellona at your side
              And join my name to one far more august.
              On outstretched wings I'll soar above
                   the frays   2490
              And rival Pallas in my warlike ways.

     [*She exits as the call to arms is sounded.*]

Scene viii

[*Enter* ROSAURA, *who stops* CLOTALDO.]

ROSAURA: I know the seething valor pent
            Within your breast attends the call
            To arms, but hear me now, for all
            Can see that war is imminent.   2495
            When I arrived in Poland just
            A poor, humiliated maid,
            Your valor was my only aid
            And you the sole man I could trust
            To pity me. Then you procured   2500
            That I'd reside—oh, heart!—disguised
            At palace, where I was advised
            To keep my jealousy obscured
            And my good self from Astolf's sight.
            He spied me, though, and now insists   2505
            On mocking me with garden trysts
            He holds with Stella every night.
            But I hold this, the garden's key,
            Which you could use for entering
            The place unseen, and thereby bring   2510
            An end to all my cares for me.
            So might my honor be restored
            By one who's strong, brave, and resolved
            To see this problem duly solved
            By winning vengeance with the sword.   2515

CLOTALDO: It's true I've been disposed to act
            On your behalf since first we met,
            Rosaura, and collect that debt—
            Your tears bore witness to this fact—
            By all the powers I possess.   2520
            That's why I urged you to acquire
            More proper feminine attire

So you'd be clad in seemly dress
When Astolf sighted you at court.
It couldn't, then, occur to him   2525
Your clothes were but a flighty whim
To turn lost honor into sport.
At just that time I moved to find
Some way to make the rogue repent
His insult, even if this meant—   2530
For honor so engaged my mind!—
Contriving Astolf's death. See where
The ravings of an old man lead?
He's not my king, and thus the deed
Should cause not wonder or despair.   2535
I'd plotted murder when the same
Urge struck Prince Segismund, who tried
Dispatching me! Good Astolf spied
This wrong and, self-neglecting, came
To my defense stoutheartedly.   2540
His noble showing of largesse
Bore all the marks of recklessness
And far surpassed mere bravery.
Now, as mine is a grateful soul,
How could I ever cause the death   2545
Of one whose heart left me with breath
And handed me my life back whole?
My care and my affection stand
Divided now between you two:
As I gave back a life to you   2550
But then received one from his hand,
To which of you do I owe more?
Which action claims priority?
Receiving now obliges me
As much as giving did before   2555
And so fulfillment of my plan,
Which once seemed certain, now does not.
I'd suffer compassing the plot
And wrongly kill a worthy man.

ROSAURA: It's not my place here, I believe,   2560
                    To sway one so superlative
                    But, noble as it is to give,
                    It's just as vile to receive.
                    So, following this principle,
                    You owe that man no gratitude,   2565
                    For anyone would now conclude
                    That, though he made life possible
                    For you and you for me, it's clear
                    He basely undermined your fame
                    And compromised your noble name   2570
                    While I've made you look cavalier.
                    He, therefore, causes you offense.
                    I, therefore, merit your first thought
                    As what you've given me is naught
                    But what he gave in impudence.   2575
                    You, therefore, ought to strive to
                        save
                    A reputation thus disgraced
                    And favor my claim, not his, based
                    On what you both received and gave.

CLOTALDO: A mark of true nobility   2580
                    Entails this giving with free hands,
                    But showing gratitude demands
                    That one receive as graciously.
                    The reputation that's pursued
                    My person holds me generous   2585
                    And honored by the populace,
                    So add to these marks gratitude,
                    A noble trait I hope to claim
                    By acting now both liberally
                    And gratefully, for honesty   2590
                    Is giving and receiving's name.

ROSAURA: You gave this damaged life to me
                    And I recall well how you pled.

When I accepted it, you said
A life lived with indignity   2595
Was no true life and so the thought
That I've received one is absurd.
The life your giving hand conferred
On me was not a life, but naught.
If you'd be liberal before   2600
You're grateful, following your fame,
As I have heard you just proclaim,
My hope is that you'll soon restore
The life you thought you'd given. Why,
If giving makes one seem sublime,   2605
Be liberal first and you'll have time
For feeling grateful by and by.

CLOTALDO: Then liberal first I'll be, for these
                Persuasive arguments declare
                Your fitness to be named my heir.   2610
                Take my bequest and seek the ease
                A convent grants, for in your case
                This recourse makes the greatest sense:
                Exchange this fleeing from offense
                For refuge in a holy place.   2615
                The kingdom presently is torn
                By factional extremity
                And such affliction mustn't be
                Made worse by one who's nobly born.
                Through this solution, I'll be viewed   2620
                Both loyal to my country's fight
                And generous to your suffered slight
                While showing Astolf gratitude.
                This remedy resolves things best;
                What else might you have settled for?   2625
                God knows I couldn't help you more
                Were I your father in this quest.

ROSAURA: Were you my sire out to avenge

This wrong, I'd suffer it as mine.
But as you aren't, I must decline.   2630

CLOTALDO: How, then, will you exact revenge?

ROSAURA: I'll kill the duke.

CLOTALDO: What's this? The same
Poor maid who grew up fatherless
Displaying such courageousness?

ROSAURA: That's right.

CLOTALDO: What moves you?

ROSAURA: My good name.   2635

CLOTALDO: Soon Astolf will claim reverence . . .

ROSAURA: He stole all honor from my life.

CLOTALDO: As king, and Stella as his wife.

ROSAURA: An outrage God won't countenance!

CLOTALDO: It's madness, child.

ROSAURA: I'm sure you're right.   2640

CLOTALDO: Control these urges.

ROSAURA: So you say.

CLOTALDO: You'll lose your life . . .

ROSAURA: It's true, I may.

CLOTALDO: And honor, too.

ROSAURA: How well I might.

CLOTALDO: What will this mean?

ROSAURA: My death.

CLOTALDO: Don't wage
               War out of spite.

ROSAURA: My honor calls.   2645

CLOTALDO: That's folly!

ROSAURA: Valor never palls.

CLOTALDO: Sheer lunacy!

ROSAURA: Or wrath and rage.

CLOTALDO: Can't this blind fury be allayed
               In any other way?

ROSAURA: No, none.

CLOTALDO: But who will second you?

ROSAURA: No one.   2650

CLOTALDO: You won't be swayed?

ROSAURA: I won't be swayed.

CLOTALDO: The deed brings with it quite a cost.

ROSAURA: I would be lost at any rate.

CLOTALDO: If that's the case, my child, then wait—
                 Together let us both be lost.   2655

[*They exit.*]

Scene ix

[*Trumpets blare as soldiers march onstage with* CLARION *and*
SEGISMUND, *who is dressed in animal pelts.*]

SEGISMUND: If proud Rome's Golden Age
                 Could view my entrance on this martial
                    stage,
                 How loudly would it voice
                 Delight at this strange triumph and rejoice
                 Amazed to understand   2660
                 A beast had armies under his command!
                 With such unbridled might,
                 The heavens could be mine without a fight!
                 But spirit, help me quell
                 These arrogant displays and not dispel   2665
                 This lingering applause;
                 I'd grieve to wake without it now because
                 To lose what dreams contain
                 Would surely bring me pain.
                 The less I hold things dear,   2670
                 The less I'll suffer when they disappear.

[*A clarion sounds offstage.*]

CLARION: Look there! A wingèd horse—
                 I'm sorry, but my stories pack more force
                 When I hyperbolize—
                 Four elements incarnate in its guise: 2675
                 Its body mass the earth,
                 Its soul the fire ablaze beneath its girth,
                 Its froth the water and its breath the air.

I relish chaos and confusion where
The soul, froth, breath, and body all can be   2680
A monster made of fire, wind, land, and sea,
Though dapple-gray of hue
And patchy, straddled by a horseman who
Digs spurs into its side
To fly upon his ride.   2685
But this is a refined
And jaunty dame!

SEGISMUND: Her radiance leaves me blind.

CLARION: Lord, it's Rosaura! See?

    [*He exits.*]

SEGISMUND: The heavens have restored this sight to me.

Scene x

[*Enter* ROSAURA, *dressed in a loose-fitting skirt, with a dagger
and sword.*]

ROSAURA: Magnanimous Prince Segismund!   2690
               Your lordly heroism shines
               Upon this day of noble feats
               From out the shades of darkest night!
               For as the brightest-gleaming orb
               Among the stars displays its power   2695
               In Dawn's embrace, restoring light
               To roses and to blooming flowers,
               Emerging crowned with fulgent rays
               Above the mountains and the seas,
               Dispersing beams, dispensing glow,   2700
               Illuming froth and bathing peaks,
               So may you rise atop the world,

Proud Poland's shining sun! Avail
A woman fraught with wretchedness
Who, prostrate at your feet today,   2705
A woman first and then a wretch,
Trusts you'll comply—as either one
Of these conditions should suffice—
Since each is more than I could want
To obligate a gentleman   2710
Who boasts of gallantry to act.
Three times already have you looked
On me with wonder, blind to facts
About my life, as all three times
My clothes displayed a different self: 2715
On the occasion we first met
Inside a cell so dank I held
My grieved existence charmed beside
Your own, you took me for a man.
When next you gazed on me you saw   2720
A woman, as the palace plans
Suspending you mid dream and pomp
Turned all to shadows and vain schemes.
The third time here, your eyes behold
This monstrous and unnatural freak   2725
Attired in female finery
Yet bravely bearing manly arms.
As you'll be more disposed to aid
My cause once pity moves your heart,
I'll tell now of the tragic blows   2730
That fate's compelled me to absorb.
I was of woman nobly born
In Moscow at the royal court.
My mother had to have been fair,
For she was not a happy maid.   2735
A vile deceiver laid his eyes
On her, a villain who remains
Both nameless and unknown to me.
His valor, though, has given rise

To mine, and being the result   2740
Of his desires, I now repine
Not being born a pagan child
So I half-madly might feel pleased
To think this man was like those gods
Whose cunning metamorphoses   2745
Into a swan, gold shower, or bull
Left Leda ravished, Danaë duped,
And fair Europa raped. I thought
I was digressing, but these lewd
Accounts of perfidy provide   2750
An overview to this sad tale.
My mother, far more lovely still
Than any woman, fell betrayed
By her seducer's gallant words
And thus, like many, was undone.   2755
The old trick of a marriage pledge
Imparted by a honeyed tongue
Beguiled her so, that to this day
Its memory dispels her joys.
In fact, the tyrant so recalled   2760
Aeneas in his flight from Troy
He even left his sword behind.
We'll leave its blade ensheathed for now
But have no doubt I'll draw this steel
Before I end my sad account.   2765
So, from their bond, a loose-tied knot
That neither ties one down nor binds,
Not quite a marriage or a crime—
It's all the same now to my mind—
I issued forth, my mother's twin   2770
And living picture when it came
Not to her comely countenance
But all her sorrows and travails.
As heiress to the vast estate
Of love's misfortune she bequeathed,   2775
I hardly feel the need to say

I've come into her destiny.
The most I'll say about myself
Is that the thief who dared despoil
The trophy of my honor's claim   2780
And left my maiden virtue soiled
Is Astolf! Heavens, how my heart
Beats quick with rage when I pronounce
His name, a natural response
To hearing enemies announced.   2785
Duke Astolf, disremembering
The joys he'd so ungratefully found—
Yes, memories of love gone by
Are just that quickly blotted out—
Arrived in Poland, called away   2790
From this great conquest, having come
To claim fair Stella as his bride,
A torch beside my setting sun.
Now who would think so stellar-made
A union, sanctioned by the stars,   2795
Could come unraveled just because
Maid Stella came between our hearts?
I, then, dishonored and deceived,
Remained forlorn, remained half-crazed,
Remained a corpse, remained myself,   2800
Which is to say, too much remained
Of that infernal turmoil lodged
Within the Babylon of my mind.
I swore myself to silence, then,
As there are trials and pains in life   2805
Authentic feeling can convey
Far better than the mouth could hope,
And voiced my grief by keeping mute.
One day, though, as I sat alone,
My mother, Violante, stormed   2810
The fortress where these miseries lay
And out they poured like prisoners
Colliding all in unleashed haste.

I felt no shame confessing them,
For when a person shares her griefs   2815
With one she knows has likewise felt
Her share of them from being weak,
The sorrow starts to dissipate
And spreads a balm upon the hurt.
A bad example, after all,   2820
Can be of use. In short, she heard
My plaints with sympathy and tried
Consoling me with her own woes—
A judge who's been delinquent finds
Forgiveness easy to bestow!   2825
So, as she'd learned that honor wronged
Could never hope to be set right
By whiling idle hours away
Or simply watching time go by,
She set me on a different course.   2830
Her sage advice? That I pursue
And hold my tempter liable for
The loss his blandishments produced,
Obliging him with courtly ways.
Now, to ensure this quest would pose   2835
Small risk to me, fate intervened
To outfit me in manly clothes.
My mother took an old sword down,
The one I've girded round my waist,
And so the time has come at last,   2840
As I have pledged, to bare its blade.
Convinced this sword would be a sign,
She said, "Set out for Poland's fields
And let her grandest noblemen
Be certain to observe the steel   2845
Now gracing you. In one of them
Your luckless fortune may well find
A sympathetic ear, and all
Your sorrows solace in due time."
I came, indeed, to Poland, where—   2850

Let's skip a bit, for why repeat
What everyone already knows?—
A bolting brute, half-horse, half-beast,
Unsaddled me outside that cave
Where you first spied my loveliness.   2855
Now skip to where Clotaldo takes
A special interest in my quest
And begs the king to spare my life,
A favor Basil deigns to grant.
On learning my identity,   2860
He urges me, dressed like man,
To put on lady's clothes and serve
Maid Stella on the palace grounds
Where I've used all my craft to thwart
Duke Astolf's love and Stella's vows.   2865
Let's also skip where seeing me
Confounded you that time at court
As I, then wearing female garb,
Appeared in yet another form,
And speak of what Clotaldo's done.   2870
Self-servingly, he now ascribes
Great weight to Astolf being king
With Stella reigning as his bride
And, to my honor's detriment,
Has bid me suffer this offense.   2875
Brave Segismund, how clear it dawns
On all this day that sweet revenge
Belongs to you! The heavens smile
On your felicitous release
From out so crude a prison cell   2880
Where you had grown resigned to be
A rock against all suffering
And beast unmoved by sentiment.
Now, as you take up arms to fight
Your native land and sovereign,   2885
I come to pledge my aid, bedecked
In chaste Diana's flowing robes

Atop a suit of Pallas's
Own armor. Draped in clashing clothes
Of genteel fabric and cold steel,   2890
I join your forces dually dressed.
To battle, then, bold general!
For it's in both our interests
To stop these banns from going forth
And set this royal bond aside: 2895
For me, so that the man I call
My husband takes no other wife;
For you, so that no gain in strength
Resulting from their allied states
Will threaten our great victory   2900
Once you've returned as prince to reign.
I come, a woman, urging you
To join the cause to which I'm bound;
But as a man, I come to press
This late reclaiming of your crown.   2905
I come, a woman, at your feet
To move you to commiserate;
But as a man, I come to serve
Beside you in your people's aid.
I come, a woman, so you might   2910
Assuage my sorrows and my pain;
But as a man, I come with sword
And person ready to assail.
So, should you find yourself inclined
To woo me as a woman, rest   2915
Assured that, as a man, I'd be
Compelled to kill you in defense
Of honor, honorably, because
In this campaign of love you've planned,
I'll play the woman with my plaints,   2920
But fight with honor like a man.

SEGISMUND: Just heavens! If it's really true
                I dream, suspend my memory!

It isn't possible for all
I've seen to fit into a dream!   2925
If God would but reveal to me
How I might blot these troubles out
And give them not another thought!
What mortal ever faced such doubts?
If I had only dreamt I dwelt   2930
Amid such luxury, how could
This woman have recounted what
I saw and seemed so plausible?
It was true, then. That was no dream.
If this is so, which by all rights   2935
Should leave me more confused, not less,
Who is it that could call my life
A dream? Do this world's glories so
Resemble dreams in what they vaunt
That even the most genuine   2940
Are destined to be reckoned false
As fake ones are considered true?
Have these so little difference
That every man must ask himself
Now whether all he relishes   2945
Around him is a lie or truth?
Why must the copy counterfeit
The true original so well
That none dare hazard which is which?
If such be life's design, and all   2950
Our splendid pageantry and strength,
Our solemn pomp and majesty,
Must vanish into shadow's depths,
Let's seize the time that's given us
And reap what pleasures may be reaped,   2955
For all we now enjoy on earth
Is but what we enjoy in dreams.
I hold Rosaura in my power;
Her beauty captivates my soul.
So let me profit from this chance   2960

To let love set aside the codes
Of valor, trust, and chivalry
That she's invoked in her request.
As this is but another dream,
Let's all dream happy things on end   2965
And rue them only once we wake!
Be careful or your logic might
Convince you this is fact again!
A dream may reach vainglorious heights,
But who'd pass heaven's glories up   2970
For human ones, had he the choice?
What happy turns of fate weren't dreams?
What man has felt tremendous joy
And not then asked himself in time,
Once memory had reviewed the scene: 2975
"Weren't all these things I witnessed but
A dream?" If knowledge like this means
Great disappointment—for I've learned
That pleasure is a lovely flame
The merest breath of air blows out   2980
So only wafting ash remains—
Let's look toward the eternal, then,
And seek renown that never dies
Where joy will not succumb to sleep
Or splendor ever napping lie!   2985
Rosaura's honor lingers lost
And it's incumbent on a prince
To see that honor be restored.
I swear by God above I'll win
Her honor back before my crown   2990
And save her name from future harm!
It's best I flee temptation so
Enticing. Sound the call to arms!
I'll wage war on my foes this day
Before the night's encroaching shade   2995
Can shroud the sunlight's golden rays
In somber black and dark-green waves.

ROSAURA:	Sire, why do you withdraw from me?	
	I would have hoped that soothing words	
	Were due my sorrows at the least	3000
	As balm for salving heartfelt hurt.	
	How is it possible, then, lord,	
	That I should go unseen, unheard?	
	Why won't you even look this way?	

SEGISMUND:	Rosaura, only honor's call	3005
	Could prompt this seeming cruelty	
	In serving kinder mercy's cause.	
	My voice declines to answer you	
	To let my honor give reply.	
	I hold my speech so that my deeds	3010
	Will speak for me in their own right	
	And shield my gaze from you because	
	No man in such dire straits can pledge	
	To aid a woman's honor when	
	She looks the sight of loveliness.	3015

[*Exit* SEGISMUND *and soldiers.*]

ROSAURA:	Why does he speak in riddles, skies?
	He knows my suffering has been great,
	So how could he equivocate
	By giving such abstruse replies?

Scene xi

[*Enter* CLARION.]

CLARION:	My lady, when you've time to spare . . .	3020

ROSAURA:	Why, Clarion! Man, where have you been?

CLARION:	Just trying to read my fortune in
	A deck of cards, confined up there—

They slay me . . . no, they slay me not—
A face card would ensure a brush   3025
With death, but trumped, would leave me
    flush
With life again. That parlous spot
All but convinced me I would bust.

ROSAURA: Whatever from?

CLARION: From finding out
The secret of your past. No doubt

[*Drumbeats sound offstage.*]   3030

Clotaldo . . . What's that sound I just
Heard?

ROSAURA: Beating drums and battle
                              whoops?

CLARION: Armed soldiers sortie from the court
To end the palace siege. To thwart
Prince Segismund's unruly troops,   3035
They'll make a stand for all they're worth!

ROSAURA: It's cowardly to be allied
With him and not fight at his side,
A scandalous wonder on this earth,
Where cruel acts flourish and survive   3040
In anarchy despite man's laws.

[*She exits.*]

Scene xii

SOME VOICES: [*Offstage.*] Long live our king's
                triumphant cause!

OTHER VOICES: [*Offstage.*] Long may our freedom live
                and thrive!

CLARION: Long live their freedom and their king!
                I wish the both of them the best,   3045
                But nothing leaves me more distressed,
                Than being forced to choose one thing.
                Instead of risking life and limb,
                I'll step aside, avoid distress,
                And act like Nero through this mess—   3050
                He never let things get to him!
                It's up to me now to decide
                What else should worry me but me.
                I'll just make sure that I can see
                The party rage from where I hide.   3055
                Ah, this is where I'll catch my breath,
                Secluded on this rocky sheer.
                No, death will never find me here
                And I don't give two figs for death.

[*He hides.*]

Scene xiii

[*With the sound of arms clashing, King* BASIL, CLOTALDO,
and ASTOLF *enter fleeing.*]

BASIL: What king has ever felt defeat   3060
                Or father harassment so dire?

CLOTALDO: Your army has been routed, sire,
                And scatters in confused retreat.

ASTOLF: None but the treacherous victors stride
                 The field.

BASIL: The battle thus desists   3065
                 To make of victors loyalists
                 And traitors of the losing side.
                 Let's flee our tyrant son and his
                 Inhuman rage, Clotaldo, flee
                 His savage wrath and cruelty!   3070

[*Shots are heard offstage, and* CLARION *falls wounded from
his hiding place.*]

CLARION: Sweet heavens, help me now!

ASTOLF: Who is
                 This soldier of misfortune here
                 That wallows at our feet in mud,
                 His body soaked and stained with blood?

CLARION: A hapless piece of man, I fear,   3075
                 Who vainly sought to turn his face
                 From death, but met it anyhow,
                 Whose final dodge did not allow
                 Him final shrift. There's just no place
                 To hide from death and not be found,   3080
                 From which a man might well assume
                 The more he tries to spurn the tomb,
                 The sooner he'll lie underground.
                 Go, then, rejoin your vast brigades
                 And charge into the bloody breach   3085
                 Where you'll be farthest from harm's
                     reach,
                 Mid clashing swords and cannonades,
                 More safe than hiding in the hills,
                 Which offer no security

Against the tide of destiny   3090
Or what inclement fortune wills.
Think you by fleeing you'll be fine
And cheat death in this way again?
You'll die precisely where and when
Your deaths fulfill God's grand design.   3095

[*He collapses offstage.*]

BASIL: You'll die precisely where and when
              Your deaths fulfill God's grand design!
              Almighty heavens, truer words
              Than these man never spoke before!
              They lead us toward a greater truth   3100
              Imparted by this talking corpse
              Whose wound is but a second mouth
              From which that trickling liquid drips
              Like wisdom off a bloody tongue
              To teach how man's initiatives   3105
              All come to naught when they presume
              To counteract the powers on high.
              Our own attempts to rid this land
              Of treachery and homicide
              Have ended in its capture by   3110
              The forces we had most opposed.

CLOTALDO: Though it is common knowledge, sire,
              That fate's familiar with all roads
              And hunts down even those who think
              Themselves hid mid these stones, it still   3115
              Is hardly Christian sentiment
              To say one can't escape its ills.
              A prudent man might easily
              Emerge victorious over fate.
              I beg you, sire, if you stand fair   3120
              To common wretchedness and pain,
              Seek refuge where it might be had.

ASTOLF: Your Majesty, Clotaldo may
                  Advise you as a prudent man
                  Who's reached a wise, mature
                     old age,   3125
                  But I'll speak as a daring youth:
                  You'll find a horse concealed within
                  The tangled thickets of these hills,
                  A fleet abortion of the wind.
                  Ride hard until you're safe; I'll guard   3130
                  The rear to safeguard your escape.

BASIL: If death fulfills God's grand design
                  Or otherwise should lie in wait
                  For us today, we'll stand our ground
                  And meet it face-to-face at last.   3135

Scene xiv

[*The call to arms sounds, and* SEGISMUND *enters with his entire
company, including* STELLA *and* ROSAURA.]

SOLDIER: Here! Somewhere mid these bosky hills
                  In thickets off the beaten path
                  The king is hiding.

SEGISMUND: After him!
                  Look under every living plant!
                  I'll see this dusky forest combed   3140
                  First trunk by trunk, then branch by branch!

CLOTALDO: Flee, sire!

BASIL: What purpose would it serve?

ASTOLF: Who holds you?

BASIL: Astolf, step aside.

CLOTALDO: Where will you turn, my lord?

BASIL: We've but
               One recourse left us at this time.   3145
               If it is us you look for, prince,
               Then look no farther than your feet
               Where we now lay this carpet wove
               Of white hairs from our snowy peak.
               Come, tread upon our neck and trounce   3150
               Our crown, humiliate us, drag
               Our dignity and reverence down,
               Take vengeance on our honor fast
               And use us as your captive slave.
               For what has our precaution served?   3155
               Let fate receive its proper due:
               The heavens stayed true to their word.

SEGISMUND: Proud worthies of the Polish court,
               Attend your true and rightful prince
               And I'll make sense of what these
                  strange   3160
               Events you've witnessed have evinced.
               What heaven has decreed shall come
               To pass is writ in God's own script
               Upon this drawing board of blue,
               Where shining print and twinkling signs   3165
               Embellish these celestial sheets
               Like gilded letters hand-inscribed.
               Not once have stars deceived or lied,
               Though one soul does lie and deceive:
               That man who'd read this coded script   3170
               To hazard wildly what stars mean.
               My father, humbled at my feet,
               Believing he could shun the rage
               Portended for me, had his son,
               Born human, made a beast and caged.   3175
               His action thus ensured, despite

My natural nobility,
My pure aristocratic blood
And all my gallant qualities—
For I was born a docile soul   3180
And gentle child—that so deprived
An upbringing and inhumane,
Debasing, brutish way of life
Would father in me beastlike ways.
Now, how was this confounding fate?   3185
For say some stranger should predict
One day: "An animal shall slay
You by and by." What strategy
For thwarting such a fate would force
A man to rouse brutes from their sleep?   3190
Or if that stranger warned, "The sword
You gird upon your thigh shall be
The one to cause your death," how vain
All efforts to eschew this end
Should seem if one then bared the blade   3195
And left it pointing at his chest!
Or if he bode, "The silvery spumes
That cap the sea shall someday serve
As gravestones on your watery tomb,"
How prudent would it be to brave   3200
The ocean deep precisely as
Its cresting waves and snow-capped peaks
Arose like mountains of clear glass?
To act so heedlessly tempts fate,
As he who wakes a sleeping beast   3205
Discovers once he's sensed its threat;
As he who fears a sword's cold steel
Learns while unsheathing it; as he
Who swims in stormy seas construes.
For even if—now hear me out—   3210
My fury were a sleeping brute,
My savagery a tempered sword,
And all my raging tranquil seas,

Harsh treatment and blind vengefulness
Would not reverse man's destiny,   3215
But hasten that it come to pass.
That mortal who, by hopeful acts,
Would influence the turns of fate
Must seek a more judicious path.
Foreseeing future harm does not   3220
Ensure the victim will be spared
Its ravages, for while it's true
That man may save himself some care
Through sheer humility—that's clear—
This happens only once the harm   3225
Presents itself, as there is just
No chance that fate will be disarmed.
Let this amazing spectacle,
These strange events, this horror show
And wondrous pageant play serve as   3230
A lesson to us all. Who knows
A more exemplary case? Despite
Divining heaven's secret plans,
A father lies at his son's heels,
A king who's forfeited command.   3235
The skies had willed this to occur
And, intrigue as he might to stave
Off fate, he failed. What chance could I
Then hope to have—a man less gray,
Less brave, less erudite than he—   3240
To alter fortune's ways? Rise, sire.
Give me your hand. Since heaven has
Exposed the ruses you contrived
As yet more futile ploys to change
Their plotted course, I humbly bare   3245
My neck to you, beneath your heels,
So you might settle these affairs.

BASIL: Our noble son, this virtuous
                    Display has fathered you again

In our own heart. You'll reign as prince.   3250
The laurel leaf and palm are meant
For you as victor on this day.
Let gallant actions be your crown.

ALL: Long live Prince Segismund! All hail!

SEGISMUND: Now that it seems my valor's bound   3255
To win me yet more victories,
I'll start with my most dogged foe
And quell myself. Come, Astolf, take
Rosaura's hand and be betrothed.
Thus will your debt of honor be   3260
Repaid, and I'll vouchsafe for this.

ASTOLF: Correct though you may be about
Such satisfaction, lord, admit
The lady cannot claim descent
And that I'd stain my family name   3265
By marrying a woman who . . .

CLOTALDO: Before you say more, Astolf, wait.
Rosaura's blood is noble as
Your own, and gladly would I duel
The man who'd gainsay this, for she's   3270
My child. That should suffice for you.

ASTOLF: How's that?

CLOTALDO: I thought it best to keep
The secret hid till she could be
Both honorably and nobly wed.
The story is quite long, indeed,   3275
But in the end, she is my child.

ASTOLF: If this is true, I will uphold
My pledge.

SEGISMUND: We've only Stella now
                        To turn our thoughts to and console.
                        Considering her sudden loss   3280
                        Of so renowned and brave a prince,
                        I place in my own hands the charge
                        Of finding one who rivals him,
                        If not superior in worth
                        And riches, then at least his peer.   3285
                        Fair Stella, take my hand.

STELLA: I've no
                        Right to the happiness I feel.

SEGISMUND: Clotaldo, loyal servitor
                        Of my good sire, these arms now stretch
                        Forth to embrace you, promising   3290
                        To render all you may request.

1ST SOLDIER: This man has never served your cause
                        And yet is honored so? What lies
                        Ahead for me, then, as the font
                        Of all this turmoil and the might   3295
                        That freed you from your tower jail?

SEGISMUND: That selfsame tower. And to ensure
                        You'll not set foot from there alive,
                        We'll station guards at all the doors.
                        Of what use is the traitor once   3300
                        The treason has been carried out?

BASIL: Your wisdom awes this gathering.

ASTOLF: He seems a different person now.

ROSAURA: A prudent and judicious prince!

SEGISMUND: But why should you feel awe or fear?   3305

The dream that was my schoolmaster
Will grieve me if it reappears
And I awake to find myself
Imprisoned once again, locked up
In my rank cell. But should it not,   3310
To dream this would be quite enough!
For on this earth, I've come to see
That all of human happiness
Must reach an end, just like a dream.
So in what little time is left,   3315
I'll seize this opportunity
To ask forgiveness for our flaws,
As noble souls like yours are wont
To pardon others for their faults.

Explanatory Notes

line 1—hippogriff: a mythic creature having the body of a horse and the wings, head, and claws of a griffin.

line 10—Phaëthon: son of Helios who was killed by Zeus's thunderbolt while driving his father's sun chariot too near the earth.

line 164—Mount Etna: an active volcano in Sicily beneath which, according to Roman mythology, the god Vulcan housed his forge.

line 227—dropsy: also called "hydropsy" or "edema," an ailment characterized by the accumulation of fluid in body parts or cavities.

line 332—giant: perhaps a conflation of the story of the Tower of Babel in Genesis 11 : 1–9 with the myth of the Titans' attempt at their birthplace in Flegra (modern-day Macedonia) to expel the gods from Mount Olympus.

line 350—sacred skits: a glib reference to the *autos sacramentales,* one-act allegorical plays celebrating the divine mysteries of the Holy Eucharist. Clarion here makes the qualities of humility and arrogance into stock characters.

line 487—Aurora: Roman goddess of the dawn.

line 488 (and lines 2491 and 2888)—Pallas the Athene: Pallas Athena, Greek goddess of war, wisdom, and crafts, born fully grown and clad in armor by springing from her father Zeus's head.

line 489—Flora: Roman goddess of flowers and spring.

line 555—God of Love: Amor or Cupid in Roman mythology, Eros to the Greeks, the blind, winged son of Venus (Aphrodite in Greek mythology) whose arrows caused their unwitting targets to fall in love.

line 580—Thales: Greek philosopher, scientist, and mathematician from Miletus (625–547 B.C.).

line 580—Euclid: antiquity's most prominent mathematician, active in Alexandria (fl. 300 B.C.).

line 608—Timanthes: noted Greek painter who flourished around
    400 B.C.

line 609—Lysippus: famous Greek sculptor of the fourth century B.C.

line 691—Our Lord was crucified: according to the Gospels Matthew
    27:45, Mark 15:33, and Luke 23:44–45, the skies grew dark as
    Jesus Christ died on the cross.

line 840—Seneca: Roman playwright, philosopher, and rhetorician
    (4? B.C.–A.D. 65) born in the imperial province of Hispania (mod-
    ern-day Spain).

line 854—Atlases: in Greek mythology, the Titan Atlas was con-
    demned to support the world on his shoulders for having led a
    failed rebellion against Zeus.

line 975—labyrinth: in Greek mythology, the maze constructed by
    Daedalus to enclose the fearsome Minotaur. Theseus found and
    slew this creature, half man, half bull, following thread he had un-
    raveled in order to ensure his exit.

line 1833—phoenix: a mythological bird, with a life span of five hun-
    dred years, that is magically reborn from the ashes of its own pyre.

line 1838–40—"Our cares are cowards . . . cravenly in packs": a pop-
    ular Spanish refrain notes that misfortunes tend to befall people all
    at once.

line 2041—Icarus: a youth in Greek mythology who, wearing wings
    fashioned from feathers and wax, flew too near the sun and fell into
    the sea.

line 2216—Plato: famous Greek philosopher (c. 427–c. 348 B.C.); his
    name here is a play on the word "plate." "Nicomedes," in the Span-
    ish original, was a Greek mathematician (280?–210? B.C.) whose
    name is a play on "you don't eat."

line 2219—Diet of Worms: the imperial assembly before which Mar-
    tin Luther in 1521 defended religious beliefs that would lead to the
    Protestant Reformation. Clarion plays on these words in a reference
    to his unappetizing prisoner's fare. In the Spanish original, the
    "Nicene Council," the Catholic Church's first ecumenical assembly,
    is a play on "nor do I sup" ("ni ceno").

line 2222—Secret: this ironic personification of a little known, newly
    canonized saint with a beatific quality of silence parodies the
    Catholic Church's updating of its already crowded calendar.

line 2488—Bellona: Roman goddess of war who followed Mars into
    battle.

line 2675—four elements: the Greek philosopher and statesman Empedocles (c. 490–430 B.C.) believed that all matter was composed of earth, air, fire, and water.

line 2747—Leda: in Greek mythology, a maiden raped by Zeus, who took the shape of a swan. Their offspring was the famed beauty Helen of Troy.

line 2747—Danaë: in Greek mythology, a princess of Argos ravished by Zeus, who took the shape of a shower of gold that rained down upon her as she slept.

line 2748—Europa: in Greek mythology, a Phoenician princess carried off by Zeus, who took the shape of an enticing white bull.

line 2761—Aeneas: Trojan warrior and hero of Virgil's *Aeneid*. Having fled the fall of Troy, he became a lover of Dido, queen of Carthage, who committed suicide with a sword after he had abandoned her on his way to founding Rome.

line 2803—Babylon: ancient Mesopotamian city considered by Old Testament Jews to be idolatrous and, thus, a place of moral confusion.

line 2887—Diana: Roman virgin goddess of the hunt and the moon (see line 682).

line 3050—Nero: dissolute Roman emperor (A.D. 37–68) who, according to legend, fiddled while Rome burned in A.D. 64.

FOR THE BEST IN PAPERBACKS, LOOK FOR THE

In every corner of the world, on every subject under the sun, Penguin represents quality and variety—the very best in publishing today.

For complete information about books available from Penguin—including Penguin Classics, Penguin Compass, and Puffins—and how to order them, write to us at the appropriate address below. Please note that for copyright reasons the selection of books varies from country to country.

In the United States: Please write to *Penguin Group (USA), P.O. Box 12289 Dept. B, Newark, New Jersey 07101-5289* or call 1-800-788-6262.

In the United Kingdom: Please write to *Dept. EP, Penguin Books Ltd, Bath Road, Harmondsworth, West Drayton, Middlesex UB7 0DA.*

In Canada: Please write to *Penguin Books Canada Ltd, 90 Eglinton Avenue East, Suite 700, Toronto, Ontario M4P 2Y3.*

In Australia: Please write to *Penguin Books Australia Ltd, P.O. Box 257, Ringwood, Victoria 3134.*

In New Zealand: Please write to *Penguin Books (NZ) Ltd, Private Bag 102902, North Shore Mail Centre, Auckland 10.*

In India: Please write to *Penguin Books India Pvt Ltd, 11 Panchsheel Shopping Centre, Panchsheel Park, New Delhi 110 017.*

In the Netherlands: Please write to *Penguin Books Netherlands bv, Postbus 3507, NL-1001 AH Amsterdam.*

In Germany: Please write to *Penguin Books Deutschland GmbH, Metzlerstrasse 26, 60594 Frankfurt am Main.*

In Spain: Please write to *Penguin Books S. A., Bravo Murillo 19, 1° B, 28015 Madrid.*

In Italy: Please write to *Penguin Italia s.r.l., Via Benedetto Croce 2, 20094 Corsico, Milano.*

In France: Please write to *Penguin France, Le Carré Wilson, 62 rue Benjamin Baillaud, 31500 Toulouse.*

In Japan: Please write to *Penguin Books Japan Ltd, Kaneko Building, 2-3-25 Koraku, Bunkyo-Ku, Tokyo 112.*

In South Africa: Please write to *Penguin Books South Africa (Pty) Ltd, Private Bag X14, Parkview, 2122 Johannesburg.*